Puffin Books
*Editor: Kaye Webb*

The Loss of the *Night Wind*

'Look,' said the policeman, 'suppose you were going to run away, would you do it that time of night, with no money and a ten-mile walk to the nearest main road? There's not a bus out of Rudharbour after eight, is there? And don't you think a lad wandering around on the Great North Road or in one of the towns late at night without cash would have been picked up?'

'Well, he could have got a lift in a car somewhere.'

'The day trippers' cars had all left by eight and nobody up on the caravan site gave him a lift. No, George Telford went out on the *Night Wind*.' And that same night the fishing coble the *Night Wind* had capsized, presumably taking all her crew with her.

But *how* could a boat capsize on a calm night, and had John's friend Fordie really been aboard, or had he run away as he had always talked of doing? However unpopular it made him, John was determined to go round asking questions until he proved to his own satisfaction what had happened, and increasingly it seemed connected with Will Martin, the efficient yet mysteriously unpopular steamship master who lived in their village.

Sylvia Sherry is an original and exciting writer who is making a reputation for herself with her adventure stories, each of them set in an interesting and unusual background. If you have enjoyed this, try *A Pair of Jesus-Boots*, also published in Puffins.

For readers of ten and over.

SYLVIA SHERRY

# The Loss of the *Night Wind*

Puffin Books

Puffin Books: a Division of Penguin Books Ltd,
Harmondsworth, Middlesex, England
Penguin Books Australia Ltd, Ringwood,
Victoria, Australia
Penguin Books Canada Ltd,
41 Steelcase Road West, Markham, Ontario, Canada
Penguin Books (N.Z.) Ltd, 182–190 Wairau Road,
Auckland 10, New Zealand

First published by Jonathan Cape 1970
Published in Puffin Books 1974


Made and printed in Great Britain by
C. Nicholls & Company Ltd
The Philips Park Press, Manchester
Set in Linotype Pilgrim

*for Ralph Elmes and James Maxwell*

# I

It was dark but thick-starred that September night, I remember, and about nine o'clock Fordie Telford and me finished up leaning against the old shed next to the lifeboat station. The sea went on murmuring against the harbour wall, and the summer visitors had gone to the pub, or back to the caravan site that was in the field next to it, or to the towns. Our part of the village was that quiet and empty – like the inside of an abandoned mine-shaft, as my dad would have said.

'I'm sick of this place,' Fordie grumbled. 'It's a dump.' Fordie was George Telford really, but all his pals called him Fordie.

Then we heard a cough and the scratch of a match from round the corner of the shed, and we realized we weren't as alone as we thought. Fordie lowered his voice a bit.

'I'm sick of it. I'm running away.'

'Ah, go on,' I said. 'You're always saying that. Where you going to run to?'

'I'd be daft to tell *you*.'

'You'd be daft to try it on.'

'No I wouldn't.'

There was a shuffling of feet from round the corner and a voice said, 'Stars is a sight too bright.'

That was 'Uncle Bob' Hymas – we both knew *his* voice. He was called Uncle Bob after 'Bob's-your-uncle' and so that he wouldn't be confused with Robert 'Tanner' Hymas, his cousin.

'Aye.' That was Tanner.

'Wind's shifting but.'

'Not over much.'

The local fishermen who'd come out to judge the prospects for the night were silent again, and Fordie said,

'I mean it, man. I'm running away.'

'But where would you go to?'

'I'm not telling that to you or anybody else.'

'Ah go on . . .'

'What you don't know you can't tell.'

'I wouldn't tell on you.'

'You mightn't mean to, but you would.'

There was nothing I could say to that. 'Rudharbour's not so bad,' I said.

'Huh!'

Uncle Bob cleared his throat again.

'Why, man, there's no point in going out the night.'

It was a kind of game they played, the fishermen, trying to put each other off going out fishing so they could sneak off first themselves. I leaned back against the shed, feeling the rough wood catching against my coat, and wondered why they bothered. And why Fordie was bothering to pretend he would run away. The men would go out fishing, and Fordie would be at school next day and nothing would change. That's what I thought. I was thirteen then and I thought I had a pretty good impression of myself and other people. I knew what I liked and what I didn't like, and I had my own opinions about a lot of things.

I didn't know it all, though. I didn't know how suddenly things could change and how much I could change,

I mean change my ideas about fundamental things. I didn't know that some of the people standing beside the shed that night would never be seen again.

'Hi, lads. The crack skipper himself!' It was Uncle Bob speaking low, and we heard firm, brisk footsteps coming towards us from Sea Lonnen, the short street of houses below Cross Point.

'Don't get in his way, man. He's a busy fellow.'

'Willy the devil.'

'Willy the beast.'

The fishermen went on, not too quietly neither, making jokes at Will Martin's expense. I'd heard them doing it before, joking, but with a lot of dislike in their voices as well. You never saw Will Martin give any sign he heard and he never said anything back. For that matter, you never saw him having a crack with the men or walking up to the pub with them. Always by himself. In any case, we didn't see a lot of Will Martin in the village, because he was master of a small steamer that sailed from North Shields, and he was generally away on a trip.

He must have been off on a trip then. His footsteps came on and he passed along by the shed.

'Off again, Will?' Tanner Hymas shouted. I couldn't understand why there was such a scornful note in his voice.

'Watch out for the black ice, Will.'

'Aye, it gets bad Amble way!'

They burst into guffaws. Well, I laughed myself. Amble was just a few miles along the coast from Rudharbour. You wouldn't find much black ice there!

Will Martin didn't answer. His footsteps went on ringing up the Harbour Road towards the place near the bus stop where he garaged his car. The houses in Sea Lonnen had no garages.

The fishermen round the corner of the shed began to move. I could hear the muffled sound of sea-boots against the paving stones, the clink of gear being carried. Shadowy forms slipped across the sky down to the harbour's edge.

One after another the little lights went on in each of the fishing-boats, 'cobles' as they are called here in the north, and moved unsteadily as the boats were got ready. Then again and again the sound of engines starting up shattered the quiet, and the roar and the little lights went steadily, fading, out past the harbour wall, over the bar, into the darkness – the *Lambton*, the *Pity Me*, the *Sea Witch* and the *Night Wind* (that was the coble belonging to the two Bobs).

'Well, I'd better get home,' I said. 'I'll have my mam shouting for me all over the village else.'

There was no reply from Fordie.

'You coming in now, Fordie?'

Still no reply.

'Hi, Fordie!'

He wasn't there. I walked all round that shed, but Fordie had gone. I couldn't believe it.

Can you beat that? I thought as I walked along Harbour Road. Going off home and never saying a word, and we were supposed to be pals! It was just as if he'd vanished into thin air. What a weird way to go on! There wasn't a soul about the village now, but there were lights in the windows of the row of little flat-faced, stone houses facing the harbour. A car engine roared suddenly at the far end of the street and I heard its engine complaining as it went up the hill out of the village.

The Telfords' house was next to ours, but there was no light shining through the curtains there. By, Fordie's gone to bed quick, I thought.

I heard voices as soon as I got in. Andy Armstrong, the coastguard, had called and he and my dad were having a crack.

'Why no,' my dad was saying, leaning forward to the fire to keep warm. 'Why no. You can't tell me it's a bad thing the pits closing. The pits finished me and many another lad I knew. It's dirty work and unhealthy work, and it's a good thing we're seeing the back on them.' And he gave us a sample of his cough.

'Aye, but what about the unemployed, man? All them men thrown out of work...'

'There'll be other jobs for them. You'll see. And better jobs. Look at all them factories along the coast road to Newcastle – for a start. Clean work that is.'

'Clean? Oh aye. That's as much as you can say about it. There's my sister's lad started in one of them – bread or crisps or something they make. You should hear him on about it. Bored stiff with it, he is.'

'Aye, well there's that. And you'll not find the spirit – community spirit – we had down the pits. But there's nowt more important than your health. *I* should know.'

And he did know. My dad had to give up his job in the mines when I was a kid because of what the dust had done to his chest. He came to live at Rudharbour because he thought it would do his chest good, and no son of his was going down the pit. 'Rather have him drownded at sea', he used to say, 'than buried alive.' Well, if it was left to me it wouldn't be either!

'By, here's a stranger!' said my dad now, looking at me

for the first time since I came in. 'Who's this then? Here, Sally – come and see who this is just come in!'

He meant me, of course, and it was his idea of a joke to have my mam shouting, 'Who is it?' and rushing in from the kitchen to see.

'Why, it's only our John! Get away with you! I couldn't think who it was!'

'Well, he *is* a stranger, isn't he? Never in the house these days!'

'Your dad tells me you're spending a lot of time on Holy Island, John,' Andy Armstrong said to me.

'Lindisfarne, man. Lindisfarne,' my dad corrected him.

'Aye well, it comes to the same thing in the end. It's been Holy Island in these parts as long as I can remember.'

'Maybe, but we might as well get things right when we can.'

My dad would argue over two flies on the wall when he was in the mood.

'I'm studying the bird migration there,' I said, to get him off the track.

'For school, is it?'

'It's his hobby,' said my mam. 'He's fair crazed about it. Nothing else on his mind just now.'

'He wants to go in for it – when he's left school. Wants to be a – go on, our John, you tell him what it is. A great long word, it is, like "chrysanthemum". Just listen to this.'

My dad would insist on going on like that – it embarrassed me, especially with Andy Armstrong, because he'd been a skipper once and he must have had a fair education.

'Ornithologist,' I muttered.

'That's it! That's long enough for you, isn't it? The things that lad keeps in his brain – let's have it again, our John.'

'Ah, Dad, give it up!' I was glad that Andy Armstrong took it all right and laughed about it.

'Well, you watch out for yourself crossing over to the island,' said Andy. 'Tides are treacherous over that causeway, and in the dark they can have you off your feet and you don't know which way to head for safety. Couple drowned there last Christmas – you mind that?'

'Tragedy it was! A tragedy. Don't worry. We've both been on to him about it.'

They had as well. You'd have thought I was about six, the times I was told to watch the tides when I was crossing to the island. As I say, I had no intention of getting drowned. They needn't have worried.

Before I went to bed that night, I was standing at the bedroom window looking out and thinking what I was going to do the next day, because I always did believe in planning things. I was going to get up before dawn and go up to Cross Point to make notes on the dawn chorus of the birds and the bird activity early in the morning. That meant I had to will myself to wake up on time, so I stood there looking out at the black space where the sea and sky were, and concentrating on four o'clock next morning. It took about a minute's concentration. I knew, because I'd done it before. From the window I could see the lights of the four cobles about a mile and a half out, spaced for fishing. I was glad it wasn't me out there really. I liked the sea, but not like Fordie did. I was always a bit nervous about it, especially on the Northumberland coast, because the storms could be fierce and the rocks were treacherous. And those cobles were little.

While I was standing watching, I saw the light on one coble move away from the rest, making up north. Looking for better fishing on the new tide, I thought. I checked the time and it was half past eleven. She would probably be going up towards the Farnes and Holy Island, north of Rudharbour. And tomorrow morning the cobles would take their catches south down the coast to the fish quay at North Shields – if they had the catches to make it worth while!

I woke up early next morning, like I'd planned. It was about half past four and still dark, but my dad was already up. He'd got the fire going and the kettle boiling. He was sitting there on his haunches staring at the fire between the bars. He always got up early. It was habit. He'd got so used to getting up for the early shift when he was a miner that he couldn't break the habit now any more than the old fishermen in the village could help putting their noses outside in the middle of the night to see what the weather was like.

'What you up for this time of day?' he asked. 'Not off bird-watching again?'

'Going up to the point. I want to see what happens when the day breaks.' I hung my binoculars round my neck and picked up my scarf and gloves.

'Have a cup of tea before you go. Never go out early on an empty stomach.'

Dad's tea was always black, strong and steaming hot, not 'water bewitched' as he scornfully called other people's brew. Made you feel better though.

The village was deserted, and it was an eerie feeling

walking past the dark houses along Sea Lonnen and then past the bulky shapes of cattle in the fields leading up to the point. They snorted and leapt away as I came past.

It was still dark when I got up there, and I found a place to settle in among the rocks by the old Celtic cross that stood near the edge of the cliff. I got a notebook and pencil ready, and while I was waiting for something to happen, I took a look out to sea. There were the lights of two cobles still there, and a big ship, well lit up, was moving south, almost out of sight, down towards the Tyne.

Already there were stirrings and twitterings all round me. A mallard was grunting, and a blackbird sang slow and softly. Then I heard the 'err-err-err' of a carrion-crow and the 'tior-tiorti' of a missel-thrush. A pair of herring gulls were crying in the darkness over the sea, and a curlew began to howl farther down the cliff below me. As dawn drew near the early risers stopped singing and the later risers took over, and it seemed to get colder then. The black night clouds rolled away to the west, the eastern sky turned yellow and jade-green, and the sea appeared again, grey and white, rolling beneath me. The lights of the distant cobles dimmed.

I was making a scientific record of all the bird movements the best way I could with a shivering body and stiff fingers; I stayed as late as I dared, which was eight o'clock, by which time the sky was light and blue and it was full day.

I stood up suddenly, and somebody just beside me gave a shriek. It was Linda Martin, Will Martin's daughter. She looked as if I'd given her the shock of her life. I suppose it must have been a bit frightening me suddenly coming up out of the earth – or that's what it must have seemed like.

'John Watt! Hiding yourself away like that! You scared me stiff! What you up to?'

'What *you* up to?' I retorted. 'I'm watching the birds.'

'Got to find some stuff for botany,' and she looked round the point as though she bore it a grudge.

'What kind of stuff?'

'Oh, I don't know. Anything that's going, I suppose.'

Linda Martin was older than me, and she was the beauty queen of the school. I suppose she was good-looking, but I didn't like her much. She was sulky and stand-offish. Thought too much of herself. Well, that could be general to the Martin family. My mam said the Martins were 'stuck-up'. 'That woman' she would say, meaning Mrs Martin, always cut her dead and so my mam always did the same for Mrs Martin.

Linda Martin had never had much to say to me, even though we'd been getting on the same bus for school twice a day for years, and now she had the cheek to stand there in her school uniform that she'd shortened in spite of the school regulations, and turn her nose up and look bored and say, 'Well, *you* know about that sort of thing. What'll I take?'

There was plenty, goodness knows. In early autumn there is still masses of colour on the point for anybody with eyes to see it. There were some purple thistle heads on the burdock plants and yellow patches of ragwort dotted about. Down in the hedgerow along Sea Lonnen there were scarlet haws. I mentioned these things to her, and she looked disdainfully at the burdock and ragwort and then, carefully putting on her gloves first, she went over to get some.

'This'll do,' she said, a piece of each in her hand.

'Your dad go off on another trip last night?' I asked.

'What about it? That's his job.'

'I know. I just happened to see him.' I wondered whether she knew the fishermen called him Willy the devil.

'Why is he called the crack skipper? Is it because he's good at his job?' I asked her.

'What's it got to do with you, nosy parker?' she retorted.

'I'm not nosy – I couldn't care less!'

I took a last look at the sea through my binoculars. There was no sign of the cobles any longer. They'd probably be down at North Shields unloading their catches at the fish quay. Linda Martin was already ahead of me as I started to walk back down the Lonnen. Tossing her long, fair hair back over her shoulders, she ignored me now, waving the wild flowers in her hand idly back and forward. They *are* a stuck-up lot, I thought. Just because Will Martin's the crack skipper!

I gave a shout for Fordie as I passed his house, to let him know I'd be going for the bus soon. He didn't answer, and I hadn't time to wait for him then.

'You'll miss the bus, our John!' my mam said as she put a slice of fried bread in front of me. 'Getting up that time in the morning! You'll catch your death!'

I hadn't time to argue. I ate fast, and grabbed my satchel and ran out, leaving Dad still staring into the fire and Mam still scolding. The bus for school was standing at the end of the street, and I just had time to leap on to it before it started. I dropped into a seat and then looked round for Fordie Telford. But he wasn't there.

# 2

Well, Fordie didn't turn up at school that day at all. I didn't think much about it then, because I concluded he was playing truant. I was sure he couldn't have run away already. He'd often played truant before when he could borrow a boat for a day's fishing or get one of the coble owners to take him out. I'd known Fordie Telford spend the whole night out on a coble and get ashore about six in the morning and go to school, without having had any sleep at all. That was Fordie for you. I didn't blame him. It wasn't much of a life for him because he was an orphan and lived with his old granny, Mrs Telford, and he wasn't all that interested in school. He was better at other things like fishing, that he could only do when he wasn't at school and when his granny didn't want him for anything.

The funny thing was, though, that he hadn't told me he was playing truant. Generally he let me know what he was doing and he would get back to Rudharbour just as the school bus got in at night, so his granny wouldn't know he'd played truant. He would be waiting at the bus stop at Ridley's corner grinning all over his face when I got back from school and saying, 'Hi, kiddar! How's the jail been today?' And he'd have his satchel with him and walk back along the harbour with me just as if we were coming back from school together.

So that evening when the school bus turned into the narrow road that led behind the piled sand dunes into Rudharbour, I woke up and started looking out for Fordie. I'd been dozing all the way home after being up so early. The bus bucked its way down the steep street into the village and pulled up at Ridley's corner. But there was no sign of Fordie Telford.

It was coming in a bit cold then with a sea fret creeping towards the village, so there weren't many visitors about, but I still couldn't see Fordie anywhere along the harbour. There were three cobles moored there, and Alfie Hymas – he was Uncle Bob's brother – was stowing tackle in the *Sea Witch*. That was his coble and he sailed her with his son who was a bit queer and never spoke to anyone. I didn't like Alfie Hymas very much because he was very bad-tempered and I hesitated about speaking to him. That evening he looked particularly forbidding, I thought, but at last I shouted across to him,

'Seen anything of George Telford?'

'Eh?'

'George Telford – d'you know if he borrowed a boat today?'

'More to think about than George Telford!' He was in a right mood.

It looked as if Fordie had messed things up this time. To make matters worse I could see his granny sitting at her front door having a crack with my mam. She'd be sure to ask where he was, and I didn't want to give him away. I walked slowly towards them, quietly, thinking I might just slip into the house behind my mam's back and avoid the questions.

But Mrs Telford saw me.

'Hello, my bonny hinny!' she said.

I tried to get through our door, but my mam was stuck right in the doorway. She turned round.

'Why, our John. What's your hurry?'

'My tea ready, Mam? I'm starving.'

'And where's *my* lad?' asked Mrs Telford. She peered along the Harbour Road looking for Fordie.

'My tea ready, Mam?' I asked again, getting desperate.

'Didn't you hear Mrs Telford? Where's your manners, our John?'

'I don't know where he is. He'll be coming,' I said.

'He's likely got himself in one of the cobles. He'll be in when he's hungry.' Mrs Telford stood up, smoothing down her flowered pinafore with hands that were swollen and scarred from years of baiting lines of fish-hooks. 'I'd better get started on his tea.'

I felt a bit uncomfortable about not telling her that Fordie hadn't been at school, but I knew he would be back soon and I couldn't go and give him away. You can't do that to a pal.

It was a bit later and we were having our tea at the table in the front window. Sausages it was, I remember. The flowers of the geraniums on the window-sill were black against the grey of the sky, and the sea sounded outside. Somehow, you always noticed the sound of the sea most at night.

There was a knock on the front door, and we heard it open – it was never locked during the day, just kept on the sneck – and old Mrs Telford shouted, 'Are you there, hinny?' and came in to the living-room. She stood in the doorway, her hand trembling a bit on the door, her face a round luminous blob in the dusk.

'Eh, I'm sorry to bother you at your teas, Mrs Watt, but it's our George. He's not got back yet and I'm sick with worry. I wondered if your John had any idea where he went?'

That was a bit of a shock. I'd been sure Fordie would have been home.

'Come on, our John. Where did the lad go when he got off the bus?'

I couldn't hold back any longer.

'He wasn't on the bus.'

'You mean he stopped in Alnwick?' asked Mrs Telford.

'He wasn't at school today.'

'Not at school? But where else would he be? Are you sure?'

Well, that was a daft question, and I didn't answer it, I just looked at her.

'Was he not on the bus this morning?' my mam asked.

'I told you – I haven't seen him today.'

Well from then on that night things went from bad to worse. Dad switched the light on Mam got old Mrs Telford a cup of tea, and they both started reassuring her. George had taken a day off. He'd maybe gone into Newcastle. Lads were like that. He'd be back soon. But Mrs Telford wasn't convinced.

'You see, I haven't seen the bairn since last night. I'm always abed before him, and he's out afore me in the morning,' she kept saying. 'I canna even tell if he slept in his bed!'

I was sure Fordie had taken a boat and gone out fishing all day. But it was a bit worrying that he was so late getting back.

I was sent out to ask about the village if anybody had seen him, but I went straight along the harbour asking the men there if Fordie had borrowed a boat from any of them. I checked everybody that had a boat to be borrowed. Funny thing was, nobody had lent Fordie a boat. Nobody had seen him that day.

I think it was then that I came round to the idea that Fordie Telford had done what he'd always said he would do, and run away. It was hard to believe he'd actually done it, but it was the only explanation of him being missing. He hadn't borrowed a boat for a day's fishing, that was certain. He might have taken a bus down the coast to Amble to fish there, but if he'd done that he would have been home by now. No, I decided, he's run away.

I was a bit stunned by that, and I started walking home slowly along the harbour, watching the remains of the sunset that burnt smoky-red above the point and feeling the touch of the sea fret on my face and wondering where on earth Fordie had run away to. And it was then that I became aware of something – a stirring, a feeling of urgency – all round me. That came first, and straight afterwards it seemed to me there were people coming out of the cottages. I could hear women's voices from doorsteps, lights spilled from open doorways across the fine rain, men hurried past me in a rustle of oilskins and a thud of rubber boots. And then the hooter from the lifeboat station came through the dusk. A boat lost at sea.

I suppose it was because we hadn't lived in the village all that long and we weren't fisher-folk, that things like that seemed to get around the village before we ever knew anything about them. If there was a grapevine we weren't on it. When I got to our house, Jane Hymas, that was Uncle

Bob Hymas's wife, was standing there with my mam and old Mrs Telford.

'Whativer's the matter, Jane?' Mrs Telford was saying. 'Whativer is it, hinny?'

'It's the *Night Wind* – she's never come back from the fishing! God knows what's happened to the two Bobs. They've been gone since last night.'

'Since last night?' Mrs Telford's voice turned thin with fright. 'Eh, Jane! *My* lad! He'll be on that coble with them!'

'Young George?'

'Aye. He's been missing since last night.'

'No, Mrs Telford,' I put in. I couldn't help myself. I knew Fordie wasn't on the *Night Wind*. 'No, he's not in the coble. He's run away somewhere!'

They didn't even hear me. They were off to the lifeboat station with everybody else, huddled in the glare of the big lights as the crew tied on their life-jackets, and Jim Pollard, the policeman, and Andy Armstrong tried to sort out what had happened.

'They're not in any of the harbours on the coast,' Andy was saying. 'And no report of them being in Shields the day. Now, lads. Let's have a bit of order. One at a time. Let's hear what you have to say. Alfie, lad. What about you?'

Andy Armstrong's voice was sympathetic when he spoke to Alfie, and Alfie was looking sad and fierce at the same time.

'There's been some monkey business out there, Andy,' he said grimly. 'I'd like to know what went on.'

'All in good time, lad. Come on now, what time did you go out last night?'

'We went out about half past nine, Andy. That right,

Jock? Half past nine, wasn't it? Half after nine. And the *Night Wind* was the first out.'

'Aye. That's about it. We went out a mile and a half and started fishing. Nothing much doing mind, and then we saw the *Night Wind* move north. That was the last we saw of her.'

'What time would that be – that she moved north?'

'Eh, I canna tell for sure. What time would you say, Jock? Eleven?'

'Near enough.'

'Aye, thereabouts.'

'It was half past eleven,' I said, and they all turned to look at me.

'Are you sure?' Andy Armstrong asked.

'I always check things like that. I was just going to bed. I looked out of the window and I could see the light of a coble moving north. So I checked the time.'

Jim Pollard said, 'Half eleven then. Not that it helps much.'

'It's a mystery what could have happened to her,' said Andy Armstrong. 'It was a calm night.'

It was still calm, but there was the mist and drizzle that wouldn't make it easy to find any trace of the *Night Wind*. The lifeboat slid down into the water and headed out to sea between the stone arms of the harbour. Andy Armstrong strode away up to Cross Point and the coastguard station, and the villagers stayed looking out to sea. As I walked back home I heard Mrs Telford's voice cry out, 'Eh, hinny! How'm I to manage without the lad?'

My mam had thought on to put the plates down on the hearth, so the sausages were still warm, but we didn't have much appetite for them.

'You're sure now, our John, that you know nowt of where George Telford went?' my dad asked, sitting down beside the fire, hunched up and gazing into it like he always sat.

'No, Dad. Honest . . .'

'Daft little . . . Eh, I don't know. It's a pity you hadn't spoke up sooner. They might have got on to the coble quicker.'

'Fordie's not in the coble, Dad. I keep telling you. If he'd been going out in the coble last night he would have said.'

'Where else would he be all this time?'

'Well, he said he was going to run away . . .'

My dad didn't even seem to hear that. He stood up and made for the door. 'I'll just have a walk up to The Rud. Might hear something.' He coughed a bit. 'Do me chest good as well.' The Rud was The Rudharbour Arms, the little pub on the hill. It was always called The Rud. My mam washed up and then went next door to sit with Mrs Telford. That left me to my own devices. So I went upstairs to the attic to sort out the notes I'd made that morning.

The attic was very small and only had a skylight, but I used it for my workshop and laboratory. There was an odd patch in the ceiling – that was where I'd blown some of the roof out when I was doing an experiment with explosives when I was interested in chemistry. I lost my eyebrows at the same time, but Dad repaired the roof and nature the eyebrows. And there was my invention in another corner. It was my idea for a mechanical window cleaner, a bit like a windscreen wiper but bigger, that I thought could be fitted to all houses and especially to tall buildings. It would have got rid of the need for men using ladders to clean windows. The only trouble was that the water supply system I'd built into it got out of control and squirted water all over the room, which hadn't made me very popular with my mam. But now I was interested in birds, and I had charts and graphs and pictures pinned all over the walls, and a special desk for my notebooks.

When we'd come to live in Rudharbour because of my dad's chest, I was just about seven, but I could remember it vividly. From living in a red-brick council house with only the street to play in or the small park two streets away, we came to this tiny village that had the sea in front of it and empty fields and sand dunes on the other sides. It was weeks before I stopped feeling strange and frightened. I mean, I'd been to the seaside before, but that was to places like Whitley Bay that were really just towns but had more ice-cream and sweets and the roundabouts and the sand. Rudharbour was different. You felt lonely and at the same time conspicuous because everybody seemed to know everything about you. And then there were the sea-birds. I'd never seen so many, and they scared me at first, but they fascinated me as well. They've fascinated me ever since.

I took out the notebook called 'Bird Life on Cross Point, Rudharbour, Northumberland, during the months of August and September 1970 recorded by John Watt', and opened it in front of me, but I couldn't concentrate on it. My mind kept going back to Fordie. It was clear enough that I was the last person to see him – well, I couldn't *see* him, because it was so dark, but I was with him. His gran hadn't seen him last night because she'd been in bed by nine o'clock. He was generally up before her in the morning as well, and made his own bed and got his breakfast, so she didn't know whether he had come home at all that night.

He'd gone off and left me without a word – and that was funny, for a start. Of course, it had been a dark night, and he could have slipped down to the *Night Wind* without me seeing him. But it didn't make sense, not if you took his character into account. For one thing, if Fordie had just been off for a night's fishing he would have told me. And he wouldn't have gone straight down to the coble either. He would have gone back home first for his sea-boots and oilskins, and then he would have come back down to the harbour, past the old shed, and if he'd done that I must have seen or heard him. I tried to think back to last night. I didn't remember any sounds or movements that could have been Fordie doing those things. Last time I heard Fordie speak that night was just before Will Martin, the crack skipper, went past the shed and the fishermen were having him on. Fordie could have slipped away as early as that and I wouldn't have known.

The more I thought about it, the more I was certain that Fordie had done it at last and run away. But if he had, it was a daft time to do it, and he couldn't have had time for much preparation.

Anyway, looking at it logically from every point of view, it was clear to me that he wasn't in the coble, and I was going to tell Jim Pollard the policeman that next morning.

# 3

'She wouldn't've got farther north than Holy Island that night.'

'Aye. But she could drift back south from there.'

'Aye. If she was still afloat.'

'Hadaway, man! Why should she not be? It was nearly a dead calm.'

'What about the rocks by the Farnes?'

'The rocks by the Farnes? Get yerself reckoned up, man. You don't think the two Bobs would run foul of them?'

It was a sunny morning. The lifeboat lay in the harbour, and the crew and some fishermen stood in the entrance to the lifeboat station, their oilskins bright yellow in the early sunlight, drinking coffee and eating sandwiches. They'd been up all night and they looked tired. A flock of gulls screamed and swooped over the harbour, hovering and swaying in an immense mobile. The wind coming off the sea was clean and sharp like the light that was filtering out of the sky.

'What fettle, lads! Any news?'

It was Andy Armstrong, just come down from the coast-guard station.

'Nothing yet,' said Jim Pollard. He was staring at a map they'd pinned up showing the coble's movements that night and the shipping in the area. 'What news from your side?'

'They've got a Shackleton and a helicopter out. And there's three other lifeboats searching. If she's there we'll find her, but we'll be lucky to find anybody in her.' Andy Armstrong rubbed a large hand over his face in a weary gesture.

'Have you got on to the steamer that went north about midnight?'

'We're trying to trace her. She was probably out from North Shields, so it shouldn't be difficult. What about this trawler you said went by, Alfie? Norwegian, did you say?'

Alfie's face was a study. He glowered. 'Aye. She was Norwegian. I'm not likely to forget her . . .'

They saw me then.

'Now then, lad, away with you. Don't hang around getting under our feet the day,' said Jim Pollard.

I knew it wasn't going to be easy to make them understand what I had to say. We were all really strangers as far as they were concerned – the Watts, I mean. But the villagers could take easier to my mam and dad than they could to me, somehow. I know I put them off because they thought I was a bit queer and what they called 'a bit above myself'.

'I've got something to tell you about George Telford,' I said.

'What about him?'

'I don't think he would be in the coble.'

'Have you been holding back information?' Jim Pollard asked.

'No. Not really. But it doesn't make sense. He would have told me if he'd just been going for a night's fishing. He always on about. But I think he did it this time.'
that he was thinking of running away.'

'So?'

'So I think he's run away.'

The lifeboat crew started fastening their oilskins again. 'I'll be getting back, then,' said Andy Armstrong, and Jim Pollard's attention started straying again to the map.

'But Mr Armstrong,' I said.

'Now, lad, I know you're the apple of your dad's eye and he thinks you're the cleverest thing ever hit the place, but we haven't time for you at present. You get off to your bird-watching and let us get on finding these poor souls in the coble.'

I was hurt by that. I've known some people call me a cheeky young know-all and take no notice of me, but Andy Armstrong had never been like that.

I watched the lifeboat set out again, rolling across the sea that you couldn't look at without screwing your eyes up because of the sun on it, and tried to tell myself that it didn't matter if they took no notice of me because if Fordie had run away he was safe anyway. I started to walk back home. The village was still quiet, but there was smoke from the Hymas's home and from Mrs Telford's, and from ours. My dad was up. The windows of the cottages by the harbour shone like sheets of silver paper.

It was a bit of a surprise to find Jim Pollard walking beside me.

'Half a minute, lad.'

I stopped, looking up at him.

'This business of George Telford saying he was going to run away. Did he mean it, d'you think?'

'Well, I didn't think so then. It was something he was always on about. But I think he did it this time.'

'What time was it he was with you on Thursday night?'

'Must have been about half past nine.'

'Did he say anything about where he might go to if he ran away?'

I shook my head.

'Any idea?'

'No, I haven't.'

'I'll make a few inquiries. See if anything turns up.'

He walked on ahead of me along by the harbour, and I saw him stop first at the Telfords' house. If he could find some evidence that Fordie had run away that night – well, Fordie's gran would feel a lot better. I was dead certain anyway that he hadn't gone in the coble.

I went out along the harbour wall, past the plaque that said the harbour had been constructed by the Rudd family back in the eighteenth century and past the cross that the fishermen of that time had scratched in the stonework to bring them safe voyages over the wild northern sea. I climbed up and sat on top of the wall, the sea slapping beneath me along its whole length and the lifeboat and a couple of cobles far out and making north. The fine day had brought more visitors than usual to the village and you could see that the news of the missing coble was spreading amongst them from the way they crowded the harbour wall and gazed out to sea. The sun came from a cloud and shone full into my eyes, and enjoying its warmth a black-backed gull strode close up looking for crumbs. It took my thoughts to Holy Island, where the old man, Holy Island Joe, would have been looking out for me this Saturday morning and wondering why I hadn't turned up.

But I spent the morning there, waiting for news of the *Night Wind*, and for Jim Pollard to perhaps bring some better news of Fordie.

Nothing came in about the coble, but after a bit Jim Pollard came along to me, standing looking up at me as I sat on the wall.

'He didn't run away, John,' he said, 'and I'll be pleased if you'll say no more about it. It would be cruel to raise hopes like that in his gran.'

'But, Mr Pollard . . .'

'Look, lad,' said the policeman, 'suppose you were going to run away, would you do it that time of night, with no money, and a ten-mile walk to the nearest main road? There's not a bus out of Rudharbour after eight, is there? And don't you think a lad wandering around on the Great North Road or in one of the towns late at night without cash would have been picked up?'

'He had money. He had five pounds in the post office. He told me.'

'He couldn't have got at that till morning, could he?'

That was true enough, and it put me off for a minute.

'Well, he could have got a lift in a car somewhere.'

'The day trippers' cars had ali left by eight and nobody up on the caravan site gave him a lift. No, lad. George Telford went out in the *Night Wind*. He was wearing jeans, and a sweater and anorak . . .'

'That's right,' I said. 'But he didn't have his oilskins . . .'

'According to his gran he did. His sea-boots and oilskins are missing. He must have picked them up before he went off. It's clear enough what he had in mind, and so you just leave it to us to find him.'

I watched him walk slowly back along the harbour wall towards the lifeboat station.

'I don't believe it,' I said to the sunny harbour and high blue sky and the old stone cottages and swirling gulls. But that wasn't what I meant. What I meant was I didn't want to believe it. But the facts were there, the facts proving Fordie must have gone in the coble. You couldn't go against facts, could you?

# 4

The old man stared at me with his fierce silver eyes sunk deep in sockets where the skin stretched and wrinkled with every movement of his great bushy white brows.

'You didn't come over yesterday,' he said accusingly.

I leaned against the wall of his small garden. I couldn't explain it to him.

'I'm sorry. I couldn't.'

'But you made a promise.'

'Well, I'm sorry. I couldn't get away.' I was a bit irritated. You could never get him to see sense once he made his mind up.

Gulls were perched thickly on the eaves of his cottage and on the wall, waiting for grubs as he turned the soil over. His hands were thin and bony as they gripped the handle of his spade.

'You should never break a promise.'

'It's all right for you to say that, but things went wrong. I can't just come over to the island whenever I want to.'

'Filled with guilt, aren't you? Filled with sin! That's what keeps the preachers in business!' Suddenly he heaved the spade up, waving it round his head like a spear as if he was just charging into battle and shouting, 'Get away! Get away! Dratted haven-screamers! Thieves and scavengers!'

The gulls leapt in a cloud into the air shouting threats back at him.

'Fools!' he cried, then turned to me again. 'You're here till night tide anyway,' he said with satisfaction. 'That's a canny stretch. You missed a lot yesterday, mind. You should of kept your promise.'

'Look, I *told* you. I couldn't!' I exclaimed in exasperation.

He went on digging. 'There was a good bit of sea fog on the island in the afternoon – there was chaffinches come in to land and blackbirds, and six grey crows.'

'I can't take anything as evidence unless I see it,' I reminded him. 'That's what we agreed.'

'And how are you to see owt if you're not here? All next week things could happen.'

'But I have to go to school, haven't I?' I demanded. 'You think I should play truant just to get the evidence?'

'Frightened of guilt, aren't you? A good scientist will do anything to get at the truth.' He stopped digging suddenly, and turned his fierce silver eyes on me again. '*You* said that. Condemned out of your own mouth, *you* are.'

I shrugged and turned away. You couldn't get through to him. No point in trying. I didn't tell him that I wouldn't even have been out to the island that Sunday if my dad hadn't convinced me that there was no hope for the coble. He said to me that morning that if she was still afloat some news would have come in about her. After all, she was fishing in busy sea-lanes, not out in the North Sea, and she couldn't have drifted long without being sighted. What he said was reasonable, but it made me very heavy-hearted. I had to get out of the village to take my mind off it, so I went to the island.

But, like I said, there was no point in trying to explain all that to the old man.

I'd first met Holy Island Joe in the May of that year, when I'd just started being interested in the island's bird life. It was a bright morning, one of those days you get on the north-east coast when everything looks as though it's just been given a thorough washing by the wind and rain and then the sun's come out to dry it and the colours are bright and sharp and deep. I was lying hidden in the dunes to the west of the island, watching the northing waders that were feeding on the flat tidal slakes that stretch from the island to the mainland and are covered at high tide. The tide had ebbed then, uncovering the seaweed and grasses and leaving pools and stretches of water. Everything was fluid that day – the grasses around me bent to the breeze, the water stretched and crumpled, and the waders – curlews and sanderlings mainly – chased and lunged and chattered as they fed. When you get involved in bird-watching on a day like that, it's funny, but somehow you stop being separate from the wild-life. You get caught up into it – the movement and activity and the feel and smell of it all. You stop being a human being on the outside looking in.

Well, that was how I was feeling, when this tall, thin figure appears out of nowhere beside me, waving its arms and shouting. I was lying flat in the grass, and I twisted round in fright and saw him towering there, black and mad against the sky. And there'd been gulls, 'haven-screamers' as he called them, swooping and screaming about him. As long as I'd known him he'd had this kind of comic battle going on between him and the haven-screamers.

At first, I was all for clearing off fast – I'd never seen anybody with eyes like that or such sudden gestures. And nothing he said seemed to make much sense, till at last he calmed down a bit, and started to talk about the birds – in his own queer fashion – but then he did make sense, and I saw that he knew a lot more about them than I did.

After that, I saw him nearly every time I went over to the island, and we got along together all right, in a way. I never saw anybody else speaking to him, or him speaking to anybody else. He lived all alone there, and I think I was the only other person ever inside his cottage.

Then one day we were talking about the migrant birds that would come to the island in the autumn, and he said suddenly, 'You'll not see much of migrants from the north. Only when the wind's from the east.' Well, I found that difficult to believe, and we had quite an argument about it. He said that the north to south stream of migrant birds, coming from Scandinavia during the autumn and flying down the east coast, only appeared on the island if there was an east wind. 'East winds and fog, lad. Fog means the birds canna keep land in sight, so they rest on the island till the weather clears.'

As I say, we had quite an argument about it, and in the end we came to an agreement that I would make a study of the autumn migration that year. I would take notes and keep records and I would test his theory. But he'd got this idea into his head that I could get to the island whenever the weather conditions were right – he didn't seem to understand I had other things to do as well.

'I'd better get out to the end of the Snipe and not waste more time,' I said now.

He suddenly whirled his spade in the air again, shouting, 'Fools! Fools!' and the gulls leapt up and screamed at him. Then he put his hard hand on my shoulder. 'Wait a bit. I'll come with you.'

I waited while he cleaned his spade and put it away in the shed. Then he pulled an old jacket on.

'Life is freakish,' he shut the cottage door behind him, 'but yon's not.' His thin forefinger directed my attention to the thorn hedge round his garden, and I saw something move among the leaves. A flash of orange that disappeared immediately.

'It's a robin,' I said.

'Aye. Comes here every year. Same hedge. It comes sudden, and it goes sudden. Like clockwork, it is. But mind, come New Year's day that bird'll be gone.'

It exasperated me at times, the things he knew for certain.

'Are you sure . . .' I began.

'I canna tell *you* anything, can I? Well, John Watt, there's another bit of information for you to set about "verifying", as you're fond of saying.'

I was making for the north end of the island, because I usually went out to Snipe Point to watch for the migrants. That meant I took the Straight Lonnen across the middle of the island, but the old man took hold of my shoulder again, steering me south towards the ruins of the Priory and Heugh Hill.

'Som'at to show you,' he muttered. I hesitated, looking at him, and swiftly he shot out his arm with the forefinger pointing. 'This way. On the Heugh.'

We climbed Heugh Hill that looked down on the harbour on one side and the sea on the other. I don't think I'd ever seen the sea so dead calm there and everything such a dull grey. It was sinister and moon-like, and the gulls that swirled and the birds on the beach looked as though they were the only inhabitants ever. Out over the skyline to the south-west was the only brighter patch of light that sent a path of white gold across the sea, and the little cross on St Cuthbert's black island was silhouetted against it.

The old man pointed out to sea. 'I saw a ship pass north along there two nights past – after midnight. And another came in from the sea and turned south.'

I couldn't see any point in that at all. 'We lost a fishing coble that night. Did you hear?'

'Aye.'

'Doesn't seem to bother you much.'

'When you've known as many men lost to the sea as I have, you'll not think it something worth making a fuss about. Get away and have a look at the gravestones in the cemetery yonder. See how many islanders haunt the sea in these parts.' He looked back at the ruins of the Priory that had been there since the tenth century, and at the parish church and the cemetery behind us and murmured, 'Fate is fickle and life is a freak and I am a freak to have lasted so long.'

Now I'm not an imaginative person. As I said, I know what I'm up to and how I stand, and I go on evidence. If there's no evidence, there's no belief. But I will say that in that peculiar still greyness, with a sea chill all around, and the old man staring out into it as if he knew personally all those he was talking about – well, I felt a bit queer.

'Looks as if a pal of mine went down with the coble,' I said, and suddenly I felt tears pricking my eyes, and my voice sounded gruff. I started desperately trying to think of something else – something pleasant, like Christmas, but it wasn't easy. The loneliness of that place, with its sense of a history of hermits and fishermen fighting in their own ways to maintain soul or body, crept through me. Like the old man said, death at sea was part of the fishing tradition and Fordie had belonged to that tradition. 'Look,' I said, gruffly, 'I'll be going.'

The old man had switched his silver gaze from the sea to me, and to avoid that searching look, I buttoned my coat up closer, pulled my cap over my ears, and turned away.

'I'll come a step or two along with you,' he said, his voice a shade kinder. 'No, this way, this way!' And he plunged down the Heugh again, a tall, lurching, skinny figure with untidy white hair and wild, uncertain movements. I followed him around the harbour and along the path that went by the south shore towards Beblowe Castle. That would make it a longer trek for me to the Snipe, but you had to humour him sometimes. He had some crazy idea in his head, but the trouble was his crazy ideas often turned out to make sense. I could never be sure.

The castle crowned Beblowe Rock, fitting exactly on the top, its walls seeming to grow out of the hill. The shore was rocky there, and the tide lapped sluggishly over the sands, and a slow breeze hovered over the scrub grass. A cloud of haven-screamers went with us, circling and mocking us.

Suddenly the old man stopped.

'What time do the seals come? What time of the year?'

'About now.'

'Aye,' he whistled under his breath. 'When the ship passed north there was silence, then, after a bit, I saw the head of a grey seal coming to the shore here – round and wet, it was. Seal-like, seal-like. It dragged itself up the beach here, and away over the land towards the castle.'

Well, to be honest, that depressed me quite a bit. You see, I'd always known the old man was a bit queer and spent half the night wandering round the place, but he'd never come up with a daft story like that before. And if he could imagine that sort of thing, then this theory he'd put forward to me about the migration of birds could be just as daft and I would be wasting my time collecting evidence to prove it.

I didn't know what to say at first. Then I said, 'Have you ever heard of seals living that far inland? Honest?'

'You want honesty? Honesty, eh? Because you think I'm lying, eh? Or me old brain's addled?' Abruptly he began stamping up and down, waving his skinny arms. 'No trust! No trust between man and man any longer!' And just as suddenly he stopped, his hand grasping my shoulder again, one long forefinger pointing to the beach. 'Evidence, man! Look at it!'

Well, I looked. And there, beyond the line of the high tide was a long rumpled dent in the sand and among the grasses. I followed the track a few yards, but on firmer ground it disappeared. I didn't know what to think.

'You saw this seal?' I asked.

'Seal-*like*, lad! Seal-*like*! Don't twist my words! Like a seal it was, grey and wet and round-headed in the starlight.' He turned away quickly. 'Straight Lonnen's your quickest way to the Snipe.'

I took the Straight Lonnen quickly. I went out as far as I could on Snipe Point, and got myself into a sheltered spot, wedged between two dripping rocks, and got my binoculars and notebook handy. From the number of seafowl about, I knew there was probably a mist out at sea, and that the old man had been right about the day before. If his theory was correct, I should that afternoon see numbers of birds that were migrating come swooping in to the island to break their journey until the bad visual conditions had moved on. It was a strange, isolated, primeval spot there. That afternoon a couple of grey seals kept popping their heads up to look at what must have seemed to them an equally strange beast. I thought of the old man's story of the grey seal, and wondered.

It was a while before I saw anything but seafowl, and then, when I least expected, the migrating birds began to appear – a dozen or more redwing and a host of blackbirds came suddenly out of the sky and swooped to the earth behind me, then came some goldcrests, and suddenly I noticed a song-thrush perched on a rock near by. It was strange and a bit magical. Last week-end, which had been fine, the island had been without these birds, and now suddenly they appeared.

It began to look as though the old man's idea was right. All those birds migrating from the north, must be flying over the island throughout the autumn, and yet they only touched down there when there was mist, and the mist generally came with the east wind. Still, I decided, I hadn't enough evidence yet. It would need many more visits, in all kinds of weather conditions, to show that what I was witnessing wasn't just an accidental happening but a definite behaviour pattern.

That day I also timed the dive of an eider-duck. It swooped down through the transparent water and swept over the sea floor in search of food, and it was underwater almost a minute.

Sitting there I forgot everything but what was happening around me. I'd managed to forget about Fordie for a few hours, and the Hymases. They didn't come back to my mind till suddenly I realized that it was getting dark. I didn't want to be crossing the causeway at night. I stood up, stretching my cramped legs and sending the bird population scattering. I turned back to the island, but instead of taking the direct Straight Lonnen back to the village I decided to walk round by the castle and have another look at those marks in the sand. As I went, the sea mist began to speed silently over the island, sending first long strands among the rocks and beneath the hedgerows and in the hollows of the fields until they gradually spread and joined up, and only the tallest rocks and trees stood out.

I was affected that day unusually by the eeriness and silence and emptiness of the place. I could hear the sea near by but couldn't see it, and the wail of a common gull, that spectre bird, came sadly from the direction of the harbour. I moved as quickly as I could over the rough ground, stumbling over the tufted grass, towards the only landmark I could see – the tall Beblowe Rock with the castle on top.

I had just about reached the old lime kilns below the castle, kilns cut into the solid rock years before and now disused, when something seemed to start up out of the earth at my feet, and rush past me towards the kilns, startling me and putting me so much off balance that I stumbled backwards and sat down on the marshy ground. The shock made me hot and tingling all over. I got up quickly and began to run, keeping the castle on my right until I reached the gate that led to the pathway to the village. It was only then I felt safe, for the mist wasn't so bad there. And it was only when I reached the village again that I began to laugh at myself for panicking. After all, what was I frightened of? No evidence of anything to make me run.

What could have passed me but maybe one of the castle's two white owls after a mouse?

But I couldn't deny, although I tried not to think of it, that what had passed me had been bigger and stronger than a white owl.

# 5

Holy Island is joined to the mainland by low, flat mud slakes and sands and a causeway that crosses them. But twice a day, at high tide, the sea covers the slakes and the causeway. At the most dangerous part of the causeway there's a small white refuge box on posts for the safety of anyone caught by the tide. Passing it, I thought how I wouldn't like to spend a night in it with the sea rushing only a few feet below in the darkness.

When I got to the mainland I turned, facing the cold swift breeze and seeing the island as just a low blur in the darkness. The place must have been just like this centuries ago, I thought, when the monks at last abandoned the island to the Danes, and crossed to the mainland with the precious Lindisfarne Gospels and remains of St Cuthbert in his coffin. The wind must have blown like this, and the birds must have cried, and the sea bubbled, as they hurried across the sands to the mainland. I pedalled fast to get home that night, glad to be leaving the bareness and bleakness of the island for Rudharbour and the warmth of our house, and that was full of the smell of baking bread, because my dad didn't believe in buying 'shop food' if it could be made at home, so my mam was doing the weekly batch. The living-room was hot and stuffy, lit only by the small lamp, that was shaped like a fish, that my dad had won when we were on holiday years ago. The green tiles of the fireplace glinted in the light from the fire. My dad sat with his back to the telly, which he 'didn't hold with', hunched up and fire-gazing, and my mam looked up from telly-watching to say, 'And where d'you think you've been till this time, our John?' just as I knew she would.

'I'm sorry, Mam. I've been on the island . . .'

'Well I don't know. You would think there'd be enough birds for you to look at in Rudharbour without going all that distance. I don't suppose they're any different there from what they are here.'

'Let him be, Sarah. We should be bonny and thankful he's took to something that keeps him on dry land.'

'You'd better have your supper. There's a bit of pie, and some buttered hot.'

I never said anything but yes to buttered hot. It was a round piece of pastry, hot from the oven, sliced down the middle with a big piece of butter inside. Smashing.

'Any news of the coble?' I asked when I'd eaten a bit.

'They've had it,' said my dad. 'Had it. Stands to reason. Terrible tragedy. Terrible.'

'Poor old Mrs Telford, she's in the hospital. She's been took really bad with the shock.'

The television chattered and sang, but the room seemed silent in spite of it.

I couldn't stay still in the house. I finished my supper quickly and slipped out without saying anything. In the passage I pulled on a coat and went outside. There was a restlessness about the village that you could feel. It wasn't quiet and peaceful as it usually was at night, and yet there wasn't any noise either. It's difficult to explain how it was. But all the cottages had their lights on, and lots of people hadn't drawn their curtains, so that the village was like chains of little squares of light in the darkness. There were groups of people on the Harbour Road, mainly women, and not noisy groups either, just standing about, waiting. Next door, the curtains had been drawn over the windows and the house had a horrible blind look.

I started walking along the harbour towards the other end where Ridley's shop was. Sometimes, at night, the village kids collected there, but I couldn't hear them fooling around tonight, and when I got to the shop there was nobody there. I stood a bit, looking at the sea and thinking about Fordie, and I heard a car door slam up by The Rud, and a voice shout something. That would be some people from the caravan site. They sounded happy.

When you've lived for some time in a small village you become very sensitive to the atmosphere of the place, and you soon know if something's happening. And that's what I felt that night. There was something in the air. And then somebody said, 'That's her! They're bringing her in!' and lights appeared in the darkness of the sea coming towards Rudharbour. Cars started up on the road behind as they were turned to face the sea and their powerful headlights lit up the water and the harbour walls. And into the light came the lifeboat with the *Night Wind* in tow. Everybody surged forward on to the small beach.

It was stupid of me, I suppose, but for a few moments I was expecting to see Fordie again and hear him explaining how he'd gone off in the coble and why they'd been lost for so long. But I soon knew I was wrong. There was nobody in the coble. There were plenty of willing hands to help pull her up on the beach, and there she lay, water swilling inside her. Already a small crowd of villagers was gathering round her, but I stood back on the road for a bit, just watching. She looked gaunt and dead lying there.

'Where was she, lads?' A fisherman's voice rang across the harbour, and one of the lifeboat crew turned from helping to beach the coble.

'She was brought up from fifteen fathoms just by the Inner Farne.'

There was no need to ask if there were any survivors. It was a strange scene there on the beach in the light from the car headlamps. Andy Armstrong went past me, coming from the coastguard station. His eyes were fixed on the coble with a strange, angry expression on his face. I followed him as he pushed through the fishermen and stopped beside the *Night Wind*. Close to, she didn't seem the same ship I'd known at all, dripping and weed-strewn as she was, and smelling of mud and sand and sea.

'What about Fordie Telford and the Hymases, Mr Armstrong?' I said. 'Have they not found them?'

Andy Armstrong shook his head. 'Not a sign. No hope of finding them alive now, lad. No hope of finding them at all.'

There was a subdued murmur of voices all round us, but Andy Armstrong and me, we didn't say anything else for quite a bit, and every now and then Andy rubbed his hand over his face. He had a rubbery kind of face, and each time he pulled and pushed it out of shape it sort of bounced back again. But it was a sign he was troubled, and I could understand why. One thing that struck me about the coble straight off was that she wasn't damaged at all. There was no sign she'd gone on the rocks or collided with anything. What could have capsized her?

'Mr Armstrong, why did she sink?' I asked. 'There's

hardly any damage, is there? She couldn't have been on the rocks, could she?'

He gave an angry grunt, but didn't answer. I thought better of saying anything else just then, but the more I walked round the coble looking at her the more puzzled I was.

'Mr Armstrong,' I said at last, 'did you know there's some things inside her, floating in the water?'

'Yes I do know,' he snapped, 'and you keep off them. There'll be somebody down from the Board of Trade any minute now to look into it.'

Looking from his angry face to the coble lying there with hardly any damage at all, I didn't take offence at what he said. I knew he was upset, and puzzled. So was I. But I thought maybe he had an idea of what had gone wrong because he knew more about these things than I did.

'Mr Armstrong ...' I began, but he groaned and rubbed his hand over his face. 'Now look, lad, we don't need the help of your inquiring mind. The thing's bad enough as it stands, and there'll be an official down to make the inquiries like I said. You just keep out of it!' and he walked away.

I began to notice then that what little talk there was among the people standing around came mostly from strangers to the village. The villagers and the fishermen and the lifeboat crew were gazing at the coble silently and grimly. Just now and again you could hear Jane Hymas sobbing. A fellow who seemed to be a reporter was trying to get some statement about the business out of Andy Armstrong, but he wasn't getting any more change than I'd got. Then a car drove into the village and stopped opposite and a man got out and walked down to us.

'Let him through – nautical assessor – Board of Trade . . .' the men murmured, and the man went up and started talking to Andy while they both stared at the coble.

Suddenly there was a struggle and some shouting from the far side of the crowd. A man's voice shouted, 'Let me go. I've got every right to tell him. My family – there was dirty work done there – he should know!'

'Now then, Alfie, now then. Calm down, lad,' the men said, but Andy Armstrong heard and shouted over, 'Let him come, lads. Let him have his say!' And Alfie Hymas, Uncle Bob Hymas's brother, went over and started talking to the assessor, waving his arms about.

Gradually, the huddle of men by the coble grew silent as the assessor talked to them in a quiet voice. The villagers watched, stirring restlessly. A hush even fell over visitors to the village as the full sense of the tragedy spread. The sound of the engine of the bus was startlingly clear as it turned at Ridley's corner and then started straining up the hill. And a fisherman said beside me, quiet, but somehow ringing, 'Whoever'd thought of this happening when we was all having a crack together last Thursday night?'

I'd never known anybody who died before, except for granda Watt when I was little, and then I didn't know anything about it except that he wasn't at Granny Watt's house any longer when we went round for tea on a Sunday. But nobody I'd known like I knew Fordie had died – and not died like this. I went up Sea Lonnen to the point and sat down by the cross in the darkness and listened to the sea and thought about Fordie and the Hymases.

# 6

'Aye well. Whatever you say, there's nowt more dangerous than a fisherman's job. Look at what's happened here. There's two men and a lad gone. Two of them from one family. And George Telford was the last of *his* family. His dad and his cousin were lost at sea.'

I'd just got home and I was standing in the dark of the little narrow passage, among the smell of coats and floor polish. I was surprised to hear Andy Armstrong there, but he wasn't arguing like he usually did. I wondered whether to go in or go upstairs to my room. I didn't feel like meeting people much.

'I'm not denying that,' said my dad. His voice was sharp and perky, like it always was when he was getting his teeth into an argument. 'I'm not denying it. And I haven't the facts and figures by me, so I can't argue, can I? All I'm saying is the mine's no picnic neither. How many were lost in the Hartley Colliery disaster? Two hundred and forty – men *and* lads! And that's not a stone's throw from here!'

'No doubt, no doubt,' Andy Armstrong sounded tired, probably as tired of my dad's arguments as anything. My mam often said I got my argufying nature from Dad.

It was a chilly night, and the passage was cold with a draught sweeping down the staircase. I pushed open the door.

'Here he is,' said my dad, turning from the fire, and

Andy Armstrong looked round, his eyes staring with tiredness and deep lines in his face. They were both drinking tea. My mam was ironing. She looked up sharply at me, and I knew she knew I was upset about Fordie.

'The wanderer's return!' she said. 'Will you have a cup of cocoa, our John?' She went into the kitchen to get it. I sat down on the stool beside the two men, and none of us said anything for a bit.

'I'll be pushing on then. Get a night's sleep,' Andy said at last. 'Thanks for the tea, Mrs Watt,' he shouted through to my mam.

'You're welcome, Mr Armstrong.' She came in with the cocoa.

'Mr Armstrong,' I said. 'What d'*you* think happened to the coble?'

'She capsized, lad. Must of went over like a paper boat.'

'I suppose you base that on the fact that she wasn't damaged by any collision?' I said.

'Aye,' said Andy Armstrong, a bit irate. 'That's right.'

I thought it over for a bit. Andy Armstrong still sat there, as though he was too tired to move.

'But, Mr Armstrong,' I said, 'how could she have capsized? It was a calm night.'

'I'm telling you she capsized! She went over fast. And you'll see – the assessor'll prove me right! And like I told you, we don't need the help of your inquiring mind!'

He sounded really vexed. My dad looked up at us in surprise. 'Aye, aye,' he said, in a conciliatory tone. 'That's right. Leave it to him.'

And Mam looked up from her ironing and snapped, 'That's enough of your questions, our John.'

Well, I was upset by that. I didn't think he was being

fair, anyway. 'Fordie Telford was my pal,' I said, 'and I've got as much right as anybody to know what happened to him. I'm not asking questions for nothing!' I was really vexed and I got up to go to my bedroom. But Andy Armstrong stopped me.

'No, no. Sit yourself down, lad.' He rubbed his hand over his face. 'By, I'm tired. Take no notice. I'm just weary. Aye, and a bit worried as well because there was something peculiar about the way that coble was lost. No mistake. But I don't believe in talking about it too much. You know how it is, people get steamed up over a thing like this and then they start blaming the wrong one for what happened. Best leave it to the officials – they look at the evidence, you see, look at it straight. You appreciate what I'm saying, John?' he turned to me.

I nodded.

'All right. But I'm going to give you my reasons for saying the coble went over suddenly, so you'll know whether I was right or not when they come to the inquiry. Now first, she didn't go over slow, because there was a coat in her that would have been floated out if she had. And second, there was no sea-boots in the coble, so the men hadn't time to take them off.'

Although his words were factual, I couldn't help imagining what it must have been like for the Hymases and Fordie when the boat went over like that in the pitch darkness.

'Now you mark my words and see if I'm not right.' Andy Armstrong stood up and buttoned up his coat.

'Aye. It's a bad business,' said my dad.

I hesitated. I wasn't satisfied at all, but I hardly dared say what I had on my mind. I did, though.

'But there was no collision,' I said. 'Why would she go over?'

'Eh, I don't know! How d'you make them like this one?' Andy Armstrong asked. 'Never lets up, does he?'

'Takes after his dad,' said my mam. 'Like a whippet after a hare, he is, once he gets his mind on something.'

'Well, I'm not answering that one, lad,' said Andy, 'because then I'd have to start saying who I think was responsible for what happened. Like I said, that's a job for the inquiry.'

The front door clicked shut behind Andy Armstrong and the thud of his feet sounded past our window as he went home. The cottages open straight on to the pavement so people's footsteps outside always sound close. My dad came back in from seeing him off. He was coughing a bit.

I had an uncle once who had a bad leg. Everything used to centre on it. If you visited him or he visited you, it was 'Mind your Uncle Alf's bad leg' all the time. And he sat with it stuck out stiff into the middle of the room, so you were always climbing over it or walking round it, and sometimes kicking it or falling over it, which would be a major disaster. Well, my dad's chest was just like that. It was the centre of our lives. You might say it kept us all alive and fed and clothed and housed us. It was crucial. The big event in my dad's life was when he had to have his regular medical for the pension he got. That was when his best clothes were got out – he generally preferred his oldest and shabbiest – and that was when his cough got worse as well. For days before, you would hear him coughing all over the village, and by the time it got to the day of the medical he was hoarse as a crow. He overdid it one year, and they increased his pension as a result, but it dropped back the year after. He said himself it was an impossible standard to keep up. Well, it was getting near to the time for his next check-up, so naturally he was coughing a bit more than usual.

'By,' he said now, 'it's coming in a bit frosty the night. Starting my chest off. Where's that cough medicine?'

'There'll be a memorial service for the Hymases and George Telford on Tuesday – at the chapel.' My mam said that between the regular thuds of the iron almost as if she was talking to herself, thinking things over aloud. The room smelt of clean clothes. My dad swallowed his medicine and shuddered.

'A memorial service – is that like a funeral?' I asked.

I could have done without a memorial service. It was lonely enough with Fordie gone without making that sort of fuss about it. I didn't have a pal at school any longer, and travelling in the bus there would be nobody but me and Linda Martin. Generally, me and Fordie had had a lot of fun on the way home. Now I would sit and look out of one window and Linda Martin would sit hunched at another. Not that I wanted to be friendly with *her*.

'Mrs Telford'll be there. I'm bringing her home from hospital tomorrow. They think she'll be over the worst. Poor soul. Not another of her family left to look after her.'

'I'll have to stay off school on Tuesday then?'

'Aye. I'll give you a note for your teacher.'

I only wanted to take my mind off Fordie, and I tried to get interested in something else. I got out my notebooks and started going over the evidence I'd collected from the island. It helped a bit, because reading over the notes and sorting them out brought back the times I'd made them, sitting out there on the Snipe. I decided I'd go out to the island again on Saturday.

'Will they not want to send some flowers, or something?'

'What?'

'His class-mates. George Telford's. Will they not want to send some flowers?'

Oh – blow! I thought, burying my head in my hands and gazing down at my notes. Morbid. That's what it was. What would Fordie want with flowers? He'd never even looked at them before...

'Well, will they, our John?'

'How should I know?'

'Well, surely they generally do in a case like this? It'll look queer if they don't.'

Just then there was a thunderous knock at the door.

'Whoever's that, this time of the night?' asked my dad.

'Is this the home of John Watt? I'm looking for John Watt,' a voice shouted.

I knew that voice straight off – it was Holy Island Joe. What on earth did he want calling on me for?

'Somebody for you, our John?'

'By, it sounds like a money knock – or the police. What you been up to, our John?'

I breathed deeply. I was furious with the old man.

'It'll be nothing. I'll get it.' I thought if I answered the door I could keep him outside, but my dad was there first.

'Sit yourself down. If there's going to be any trouble, *I'll* deal with it.'

Another minute and the old man was standing in the middle of the kitchen, tall and lean, in sea-boots and oilskins. 'Evening, missus,' he threw at Mam, and then he fixed me with his silver eyes. 'You'll have to come over to the island, John Watt. Tomorrow.'

'Oh honestly,' I said. 'How can I come to the island? It's a school day.'

'You'll have to come. It's very urgent. I wouldn't have came all this way to tell you if it hadn't been, would I?'

'How often do you take telling? I can't come because I have to go to school. I can't come till Saturday.'

'I'm telling you, lad – it's urgent!'

'And will you go and explain to the headmaster that I'm not at school because you said I had to go to the island?'

We were both getting angry, and the old man suddenly whirled round and stared at my dad. Dad dropped back in his chair and started to poke the fire up. My mam and dad must have thought it very queer, me and this stranger having a ding-dong battle in the middle of the living-room.

'You could maybe explain what this is all about,' said my mam.

She meant me, but she looked at the old man as well. He just kept on staring at Dad, and Dad was uncomfortable, I could see.

'I'd better explain,' I said. 'Look, this is the man from Holy Island that I go to see – he's interested in birds, like me, and we're working on a theory . . .'

'Joe's the name,' he broke in. 'People call me Holy Island Joe. Doesn't worry me. I've lived there as a lad and as a man, and always a fisherman. I came down here the night in my own boat.' His thin hand with the fine wrinkled brown skin stretched across it fell on my mam's shoulder and made her jump. 'How old would you say I was now, hinny?'

'Eh, I'm never any good at guessing ages!' she protested.

'How old? Haway now – how old would you say?' He turned his gaze on Dad again, and Dad, embarrassed and just to make sure he didn't put his foot in it, said, 'Well now, you'll be over fifty, eh? Ha, ha! Aye, well, say sixty-five?'

'Eighty!' the old man declaimed. 'Eighty! And still a fisherman – and I can see more going on in the world of nature with these old eyes than yon lad can.'

'Ah come off it, Joe,' I said. 'I've got to prove that theory of yours yet.'

'Look, lad,' he said, leaning forward and speaking low, 'I'm not having you on. You have to come, John Watt. There's a new migrant – a new one. Very special. You have to come and see.'

'New? You mean a new species for the island?'

'I'm saying nothing more – you just mind what I said. Seal-like. Seal-like. You remember?'

'You mean it's a seal?'

'No, no – seal-*like*.' He threw his sou'wester suddenly on the floor. 'Will you come tomorrow?'

'Now then, Joe,' said Dad, 'don't worry the lad.' I could see my parents were befogged by the whole conversation. 'He's got his school work. And these nights are drawing in – he can't be crossing that causeway except in daylight.'

The old man picked his sou'wester up. 'I'll go then. But you mind this, John Watt. I warned you! Aye. If you miss it – you had your warning. The full guilt is yours! The guilt, the sin that keeps the preachers in business! Second time I've had to tell you that!'

Mam drew in a sharp breath at that and tut-tutted, but Dad said, 'Why not have a cup of tea before you go, Joe?'

'Haven't the time,' and he gave me one last fierce stare

and with a sudden turn he was gone and the front door slammed behind him.

'Well! If that doesn't beat everything,' said my dad.

'I'm not sure I like the idea of you having anything to do with that man,' said my mam.

I thought things over for a few moments, wondering what the old man thought he was up to. Must be off his rocker, I thought. What was he on about? Migrant? What migrant? I couldn't leave it like that. If I could have a talk with him alone, I might get some sense out of him.

I jumped up and ran outside, but already there was the putter of an engine in the harbour, and the old man's boat was moving out to sea. I took a last look at the wrecked coble that lay in the moonlight alone on the sand. Then I went back inside.

I thought that if I went straight up to the attic I might avoid a lot of questions, but it was no good. The door to the passage opened and Mam said, 'Come on in here, our John, and you tell us who that old man is and what he's up to. He sounds daft to me.'

'He's just an old fisherman,' I said. 'He's interested in birds, like me. That's all.'

'And what's that got to do with him coming here this time of the night and going on like that?'

'I'm not sure. He's a bit queer sometimes, but you generally find there's something in what he says. I just don't know. He seems to have seen a new kind of bird on the island.'

'Well, I've come across some queer things in my time but that beats all. Do you mean to tell me you've been away on that island associating with a mad creature like that?'

'He's not really mad. Honest, Mam. I know he sounds crazy, but when you get to understand him he talks a lot of sense.'

It was quite clear that Joe had made a bad impression on my mam. And I knew if she went on about it she'd soon get round to the conclusion that I wasn't to go on the island again. I thought the best way to stop her doing that was to end the conversation somehow, but my dad did it for me.

'I don't know,' said my mam, 'what do *you* think?'

'Me?' said my dad, and started to cough. 'All this excitement – started my chest off. I'm going to bed.' Which he did. And I followed pretty quick and left my mam to come to her conclusions by herself, so that she couldn't pass them on to me.

# 7

'The man who thinks he can satisfy everybody is a fool.' That's what my dad said once after one of his medicals when they'd lowered his pension a bit. It was because he'd cracked a joke, he said, and the doctor took it as a sign he was getting better. Not much of a joke either. When the doctor asked him what he thought was wrong with him, he replied, 'It's the mining-gitis, doctor.' He never cracked a joke with a doctor again.

But I couldn't satisfy everybody, that was certain. I couldn't be at school and on the island and yet I couldn't get the old man out of my mind. At school, everybody wanted to hear about the coble and about the arrangements for the memorial service. I just wanted to puzzle over Joe's visit. He wouldn't have come specially to see me like that if it hadn't been urgent. To my parents it might just have been a madman's visit, but when you knew Joe and you discounted his crazy chat and his arms waving about and all that, you knew there was something behind it. A migrant, he said. It just didn't make much sense that some new migrant would have appeared. But he must have seen something, I was sure of that. I decided I would go on Saturday and say nothing to anybody about it.

Monday teatime they brought old Mrs Telford home from hospital. Poor old soul. She'd been a cheerful old woman, always ready for a joke and a chat. Now she was bent and shaky, and my mam had to help her into the house. She was staying with us till she got on her feet. My dad and me had brought her bed in from next door and put it up in our front room.

You never know what to do times like that, and I was standing in the living-room when she came in, not knowing whether to be cheerful or just keep quiet. She'd already been upset seeing the coble beached out there and as soon as she saw me she started to cry. I reminded her of Fordie. I wished I could do something to help. But there was nothing I could do. Fordie had gone, and that was that.

I went out to the back garden where my dad was digging.

'Old Mrs Telford's come,' I said.

'I'll be in in a second. Is she bearing up?'

'She's drinking some tea.'

'Oh aye.'

I hung about the garden for a bit. It was a small place with a straggling hedge, but my dad managed to get some vegetables out of it. In fact, except for a narrow strip of grass and some lanky michaelmas daisies there was nothing but vegetables.

It was quite a mild evening, and I saw one stray cabbage white fluttering about. A crowd of sparrows came swooping in from the fields beyond and settled on the roof, and I heard a linnet calling in the garden next door.

Dad stopped digging suddenly and started coughing. 'I'll have to give this up,' he said. 'It's too much for me.'

I wished his medical was over. The tension that built up before it was always the same – wore us all out, it did.

'Hi, Dad,' I said, 'are you going to the service tomorrow?'

'Why aye, son.'

'Well, we're not chapel, are we?'

'You have to show respect for the dead. They were all friends in a way, weren't they?'

I went inside again. I didn't want to go and sit with Mrs Telford. I didn't know what to say to her. So after tea, I slipped off outside to walk round the harbour, and my dad must have been feeling the same, because after spending teatime saying things like, 'Eat up, now, missus. Here, have another bit of cake, hinny. You've got to keep your strength up for the morrer. More tea, missus? Come on, plenty more where that came from,' he disappeared without a word up to The Rud.

But it wasn't very pleasant in the village that evening. The village kids were playing round Ridley's shop at the corner, one or two visitors lingered along the harbour wall, and some fishermen were busy with their nets, but the beached *Night Wind* couldn't be ignored, and the more I looked at her the more unhappy I felt.

There was the sound of crunching, swift steps on the Harbour Road behind me, and I turned and saw Will Martin coming back from his trip. Seeing the coble on the beach he stopped beside me – a square, dark figure in his sea uniform – staring at her.

'They found her then? The *Night Wind*?' he said to me.

That surprised me. Will Martin had never spoken to me before.

'They brought her in last night,' I said.

'Any survivors?'

'No.'

He didn't stay long. He turned his face from the coble

and went striding on towards Sea Lonnen. I remember thinking what a queer, hard fellow he must be not to show any interest, not to go on to the beach or ask what had happened, hardly giving a look at the coble. But then I don't suppose he'd ever had much encouragement to take an interest in the affairs of the village. But I was pleased he'd spoken to me. I'd always admired Will Martin, not that I knew him, mind, but he seemed to me to be strong. I mean, he was a strong character. He didn't need to be always with people, and he always stood up straight, and he walked steadily and firmly. You could trust a man like that. At least, that's what my opinion was.

I stayed out till old Mrs Telford had gone to bed, then I went in and found my mam sitting in front of the telly.

'Fine lot of menfolk I've got,' she said, 'sliding away out of things.'

'Well, there was nothing we could do.'

She sighed and got up to switch the telly off. 'No, there's nothing much a body can do times like this. Poor old soul, she's not feeling very clever yet. I'm bonny and thankful your dad never took to the sea.'

'Hi, Mam, do I have to go to this service tomorrow?'

'Do you *have* to? Well what a question! I thought George Telford was your best friend? Some folks forget fast!'

'But what good does it do?'

'Never let me hear you talking like that again! What good does it do!'

There was the sound of a cough outside the front door. 'That'll be your dad,' my mam said. He'd come home early, rubbing his hands and saying it was coming in colder.

'There's going to be trouble,' he said, sitting down in his usual chair. 'Aye, there'll be trouble. It's in the air – just like when there was a strike about due at the pit.'

'I'd have thought we'd had enough trouble,' said Mam.

'Ah – it's not over yet.'

But it is, I thought, as far as the Hymases and Fordie are concerned – all over.

'There's poor old Uncle Bob's beer tankard hanging above the bar at The Rud. He would never drink out of owt else. And they say it'll stay there in memory of him.'

My mam made her usual sounds of distress and approval, but all I could think was that it was morbid. Like I said, I'd made up my mind about quite a lot of things at that time, and I didn't approve of being morbid and remembering unhappy things and keeping things – material objects – to remind you. I had a pretty good impression of the modern world – that it was different from the past – I mean it was different scientifically and that sort of thing, and so you had to get rid of the old sentimental ideas that belonged to the past. That's what I thought then. I still think it's a good theory.

So I went on with my work, trying not to listen, not to think about Fordie and the Hymases.

'Listening to them talking in the pub, it looks as if they know what happened to the coble and who are responsible, as well.'

I looked up when he said that, and he looked at me.

'Well, I don't say I go all the way with them, and Andy Armstrong's being very cagey about the whole thing. But I don't know. It seems to make sense. And you would expect them to know their own business.'

'What are they saying, Dad?' I was curious.

'I know from my own experience in the pit,' he went on. 'You mind, Sally, when Geordie Harrison was killed in that cave-in in the big vein, I said straight off – faulty pit-prop. And I was proved right.'

'Ah, come on, Dad,' I said, leaving my notes and sitting on the stool by the fire. 'What are they saying?'

'Well, they claim that these cobles don't go over easily. According to Alfie Hymas you would need a crane to do it.'

'They've got good stability,' I said. Fordie had said so, many times.

'That's just his very words – good stability. But according to what I could gather, there's one danger they're always facing out there, and that's if another ship comes along too close, it can cut their nets for them ...'

'I know about that. But that wouldn't turn a coble over.'

'You know all this, eh? You're with me up to now? Well, according to them, it *could* turn a coble over. If the nets got caught up in a propeller, the coble might be drawn along and swamped, understand? Especially if she had nylon nets. Andy Armstrong won't say much one way or the other, because he says they should wait for the inquiry, but even he admits that nylon nets could be twisted into a rope and if you weren't sharp about cutting them free – well, it'd be a bad lookout.'

'So they think some ship fouled her nets?'

'That's about it.'

'Which ship?'

'Well now, that's the tricky part, and Andy Armstrong's dead against it, but they say they know which ship it was. The *Pity Me* had her nets fouled the same night and they say it was a trawler did it – a foreign trawler. Norwegian.'

'But the skipper of the trawler would have known. He would have turned back to look for survivors – and he would have reported what happened,' I objected.

My dad didn't say anything to that at first. He sat looking reflectively into the fire.

'Well, he would, wouldn't he, Dad?'

'I don't know, son. It's what you would expect him to do. But there might be reasons – good reasons so far as he was concerned – for saying nowt about it.'

Ten o'clock next morning saw us walking slowly up the hill past the herring curing-shed to the chapel. Mrs Telford walked between my mam and dad, helped along by them. The fishermen and their wives joined us, everybody in dark clothes and with dark, sorrowful faces. A bus came down the hill to the harbour and Fordie's classmates from school got out of it and walked past us in a long double line. They looked at me as they went as if I'd got two heads and they'd only just realized it. I suppose they thought I was an important part of the proceedings. Fordie had been in the class ahead of me, but I did know a few of the people in his class. Jane Hymas came up to us as we reached the chapel and took Mrs Telford's hand.

And it was a blue September day with a sky full of gulls, and a sea full of white breakers, and a racing wind. But we went out of that into the stark box of the chapel that was all hushed, sickly green and reddish-brown varnish. The atmosphere of sorrow closed round us as we took our places in the pew the Telfords had always used. Only old Mrs Telford left. She sat staring ahead, not seeming to see anything.

Well, I was thankful enough when they got the service

started, but it went from bad to worse what with doleful hymns about the sea, and then the preacher starting to talk about the men and the boy who had lost their lives. The feeling of sorrow got so intense in that place that you couldn't fight it off, and I didn't want to start crying like a girl. I looked round desperately for something to take my mind off it, but the only thing I could see of interest was a plaque on the wall above the pew. And that wasn't all that cheerful:

Sacred to the memory of
David Telford and his nephew Richard Telford
who were lost at sea in the trawler *Northumbrian Maid*,
November 1961

That was Fordie's father and cousin, I knew, but nobody had ever told me they had both sailed in trawlers and been lost in one. Now they would add Fordie's name, I supposed. And as I looked round I realized there were a couple of other plaques to men who had died in the same trawler, the *Northumbrian Maid*. There was one of them a Hymas as well. That must have been a tragedy to the village when the *Northumbrian Maid* was lost, I thought, and yet nobody had ever said anything about it to me, not even Fordie.

As we stood up for the last hymn, I glanced round and saw Will Martin's wife looking across at the same plaques with a strange expression on her face. Linda was beside her, holding a hankie to her eyes as though Fordie had been her dearest relative, and Will Martin stood there, straight and stern, gazing ahead over his hymn book.

By, it was a relief to get out of there and into the fresh air. The women seemed happier after it, but the men gathered about in groups. They all seemed angry and were discussing something very seriously. In fact one of them almost knocked me over moving from one group to another, and he never saw me yet!

The boys from Fordie's class were collected together and started to walk down from the chapel to the bus that waited at Ridley's corner. They were going back to school, and I suppose I should have gone with them, but it wasn't my class and the teacher never thought of including me, so I kept quiet and out of the way. I didn't feel a bit like school that afternoon.

I went over to listen to the discussion, standing beside Andy Armstrong because he had the biggest group round him, and from where I was standing I saw Will Martin come out of the chapel and stop a minute in the porch, casting his eye over the crowd a bit like a skipper on the bridge looking down to calculate how things are going on deck. Then he moved out of the porch and stopped to light his pipe, his eyes gazing out from the breezy headland towards the sea.

It was Alfie Hymas who seemed the most worked up.

'Aye, but you'll grant that, Andy? You'll grant that, won't you? You'll grant it was some ship passing that night must have been responsible?'

'You can't say anything for certain till the inquiry, Alfie. You can only say it looks very much like it,' Andy was trying to soothe him down.

'A-a-h!' Alfie sounded disgusted. 'Hadaway, man! Are you going to hum and haw there about regulations when it's your pals have been done in? If you can't come out for your pals it's a bad lookout. I lost a brother and a cousin in the *Night Wind* and I want to know why!'

'Here, he's right there, Andy!'

'Aye, we've no time for anybody half-hearted in this matter!'

'There's no getting round the facts, Andy!'

'And the facts', said Andy, 'is only that we think her nets were caught up by another ship passing.'

'No, no. Come on now. No turning a blind eye! What happened to the *Pity Me*? Eh? What happened to her?'

'But you've no proof it was the Norwegian cut her nets!'

'I have,' that was the owner of the *Pity Me*. 'I saw her go past. Yelled at her. It was the Norwegians all right.'

'It's time something was done. It's been going on long enough – we've all had nets cut by ships coming too close and taking no heed of signals. It had to come to a tragedy sometime.'

'Aye – and who'll be the next to go?'

I could see Andy was getting more and more harassed, and it looked as if the men were really working themselves up to something. They usually took a good bit of notice of what Andy said, because they thought a lot of him in the village. He'd been a very experienced skipper before he retired and took over the coastguard station, and he was a fair man and had good judgement. He was the only one in the village I'd ever seen talking to Will Martin, and I'd never heard him say anything nasty about Will. But he was losing his hold on the fishermen now.

Maybe it was no business of mine, but it seemed to me there was a mistake in their thinking and if I pointed it out it might help Andy Armstrong.

'You can't draw that conclusion from those facts,' I said. My remark came at a moment of silence or they would never have heard me. As it was, I might as well have been talking gibberish, because their faces just looked blankly at me. 'You can't conclude', I said a bit louder, my voice going squeaky with nervousness, 'that because the Norwegian trawler cut the *Pity Me*'s nets that she also cut the *Night Wind*'s nets.'

That rattled Alfie Hymas. 'What do you know about it, John Watt?' he asked. 'What's it to do with you anyway?'

'He's got a point, though,' said Andy Armstrong, and I saw Will Martin look in my direction and then away again. He'd heard what I said. 'Tell them what you had in mind, John,' said Andy.

'Well,' I said, 'What time did the trawler cut the *Pity Me*'s nets?'

'Eh? What's that to do with it?'

'It could be important.' They'd all stopped shouting and were looking at me as though they couldn't believe their eyes.

'I can't remember. Think I took a time-check?'

'Well, was it before or after the *Night Wind* went north?'

'It were after. After.'

'Then it couldn't have been the same ship cut your nets and sent her under.'

'And how do you work that out?'

'Well, what you're saying is that the Norwegian trawler passed the *Night Wind* to the north of the *Pity Me* and sank her and then went on and cut the *Pity Me*'s nets. But if that had happened, the *Night Wind* would have been found capsized just north of Rudharbour and not as far north as the Inner Farne. And if the *Night Wind* was moving north when the Norwegian ship passed she wouldn't be fishing anyway, would she? So her nets couldn't have been cut then.'

There was a moment's uneasy silence, then a roar of derision.

'Listen to that!'

'What does he know about it, a lad like him?'

'He's got a point. After all, he's getting a better education than any of us got, and he's been trained to think things out,' insisted Andy. 'Think it over!'

But they wouldn't.

Andy walked away down to the village, and most of the fishermen started over towards the pub, still arguing and angry. They weren't convinced.

There was only Will Martin and me left standing on the path between the gravestones. He turned and looked at me and nodded. I was surprised, but I felt pleased as well that he'd noticed me. I nodded back and began to walk down towards the village, and I could hardly believe it when he caught up with me.

'Lot of excitement that'll come to nothing,' he said. 'What can they do? It's over and done with. When a thing's over and there's nothing to be done about it, it's best to forget it.'

I felt he was right. I'd felt that about Fordie. I couldn't bring him back. I had to forget. I thought I would go off to the island and see what the old man was on about. I would try to forget.

Will Martin stopped, pointing with his pipe out to sea.

'See that?' he asked, indicating a ship that moved slowly across the blue band of water. '*British Monarch*. Bound for Scandinavia. Fine ship.'

The breeze tossed the smoke from his pipe across my

face. It smelled sweet and strong. Up there on the hill, it was sunny and breezy and quiet now, and down by the harbour some of the men still gathered, talking and gesticulating, and the *Night Wind* lay keeping her secret.

More than anything, I felt very flattered that Will Martin was bothering to take any notice of me.

'That was quite a point you made about the Norwegian trawler,' he said. 'Quite a point.'

'Just a matter of common sense.'

'Trouble is, if they start thinking, they'll start accusing every other ship in the area that night. Probably best to let them go on thinking it was the Norwegians. The Norwegian trawler will be out of Shields again soon, and no harm will come of it.'

He didn't say much more, and at the foot of the hill he nodded and left me, going towards his car. I must say I felt pleased about it. I decided that he must have been impressed by what I'd said about the Norwegian trawler to speak to me like that. Yes, I was pleased all right.

I started running along towards our house. I'd decided to go to the island for the afternoon. As I ran, I thought about Will Martin and I wondered how he could put up with the nasty comments the fishermen made about him. He *must* be strong-minded, I thought, to hear them and say nothing – not let it affect him at all. I couldn't have done it.

I remembered when we'd first come to Rudharbour and I'd started at the junior school in the village, what a time the other kids gave me. I hadn't any friends then, and they used to take the mickey shouting at me, 'What, John Watt? Not what, John Watt! Which what, Watt? What not, John Watt!' And then when I'd first had to wear spectacles they'd all called me Specky and Four-eyes and sometimes hadn't let me play with them, saying I couldn't see properly. That had made me miserable. I'd broken the spectacles fighting a boy who shouted names at me. But I couldn't see any of the remarks he heard upsetting Will Martin. And I wondered why he was disliked in the village, a man like him.

'Our John! Why haven't you gone to school?' my mam exclaimed when I went home.

'I missed the bus. Well, it's no good thinking about it now, I couldn't get in to Alnwick.'

I've never seen her so put out by anything. She seemed so surprised by me not being at school that she couldn't think of any plan to get me there.

'I'm going out,' I said.

'What about your dinner?'

'I'm not hungry.'

'Take your best suit off, then!'

I dashed upstairs, got my old clothes on, picked up my notebooks and binoculars, and was off. I would take Will Martin's advice. I would put the tragedy of the coble behind me. It would be fine to be on Holy Island a day like this!

# 8

The old man was sitting on a bench in front of his house, staring straight up into the sun with silver eyes. He was so still, a gull had settled on the bench-back beside him and was looking at him.

'I'm here,' I said.

He stood up quickly and the gull screeched and swooped off. 'Never! I thought you'd given up! By, life's full of surprises!'

He always seemed to say the wrong thing. Sarky he was.

'Well, I'm here, aren't I?'

'You should have come straight away.'

'Look,' I said. 'I'm off to the Snipe. It's a smashing day and if you're right there shouldn't be a migrant in sight.'

'What about the new migrant?'

'Well, come on then. Let's get going. Where'm I likely to see it and what's it like?'

'Plenty of time, John Watt.'

He sounded more serious than I'd ever known him be before, and he took his time pulling on his jacket and joining me in the lane. I wanted to go along to the Straight Lonnen but he insisted on taking the road to Beblowe Rock and the castle. He hadn't much to say as we went, except for an occasional mumble to himself, but we were accompanied most of the way by a cloud of wraith-like common gulls that seemed to mock us.

By the shore, before you get to the castle, there was Joe's boathouse. That's what he called it. It was really an old herring boat that had been turned upside-down, and Joe stored a lot of tackle and junk in it. He stopped there now and opened the door.

'We'll bide here a while,' he said. He brought a couple of old chairs to the entrance and sat down on one of them.

'But, Joe,' I complained, 'I've got to get to the Snipe. I can't waste time sitting here.'

'You'll not be wasting time sitting looking out over the sea, John Watt. Not you, especially. Might help you to understand your own insignificance.'

I sat down then. He was in a funny mood. He sat there with his pipe in his hand gazing out to sea, occasionally making a swipe at a haven-screamer. Somehow or other, I sensed that he was disturbed, that something very significant had happened, and that he felt it would lead on to other and more disturbing events. Because of that, I sat quiet and listened to him, knowing he'd get around to telling me what had happened eventually. For a while he talked about the past, and about shipwrecks he'd known when he was a boy on the sands near the island, and how men and women had driven their horses and carts out at low tide to help get the ships off and the money they'd made out of it. But then his mood changed.

'Beached,' he said, and he sounded bitter and I'd never heard him sound bitter before. 'Beached, that's what I am, like this old herring boat of my father's.' He tapped the wood of the boathouse. 'Upturned on the beach and the bows cut through to make a storeroom for a lot of useless tackle and a shelter for an old man – beached like she is. All we're fit to be now – old monsters from the past to joggle the imagination of visitors. Make them realize there might have been things worth something in the past.'

I looked at him, at his sharp old face and his angry stare over the sea, and he turned to me suddenly. 'Aye. Take a good look. I'm an old craft you'll not see around much longer, beached or not. But I'm not the kind of old fool that goes about getting a shilling or two mumbling to city folks that laugh behind his back. Mind that, John Watt! You're too young – and too ignorant in spite of all your conceit . . .'

'Now, look . . .'

'Aye – conceit! You canna deny it. You canna understand though what I'm on about. You'll have to travel the same eighty-odd years and be looking back over the chart – like me. And by that time, John Watt, I'll not be here, so there's *one* point where you and me can never see eye to eye.'

I think I did understand, though, gazing out over the same sea with him, but knowing that while I saw the future stretched out there, he saw only the past. No good trying to explain that to him. So I tried to change the subject, take his mind off thoughts and ideas that were making him unhappy.

'You sailed in trawlers, didn't you?' I asked him.

'Oh aye. I was mate for a time in trawlers sailing out of Shields.'

'You never got to be skipper?'

'Skipper?' He gave a wide contemptuous wave. 'Who wants to be skipper? I had a skipper's ticket, but I stayed with the deckies as a mate. Aye. Turned down the offers of taking out a trawler even though they had their eyes on me for it. I was young then, but I wasn't daft – and I'm not daft now.'

'Well, what's wrong with being a skipper? I would rather be a skipper than a mate. Rather have a ship of my own ...'

'What do you know about it?' he asked indignantly.

'Well, all right. I know nothing. But I'm just saying, it seems to me ...'

'If you know nowt about it, shut up about it. The skipper's the man in the glass cage – a man apart. And if he wants to stay there, he has to take risks. And his crew curse him for it, but they curse him again if he doesn't get the catches and the money doesn't come in. He's all alone in the glass cage.'

'I'd have thought,' I said, 'that that was an extreme point of view.'

'You know nowt about it! A skipper of a trawler's obsessed – he's pursued by the things he's pursuing – the fish on the floor of the sea. The silver prize. Aye. One trip we were chipping ice off the bridge top every three hours. And shovelling solid snow on the boat deck. And the crew cursed the old man that was up there in his glass cage. But on the way back, the skipper got drunk in his cabin and they carried him off on a stretcher.'

'I suppose they are under a strain,' I started to say, when he cut in.

'Smug. That's your trouble, John Watt. Smug.'

He stood up, pointing towards the gate that led to the path to the castle.

'The migrant's along there. You'd best go by yourself if you want to get close. It would take off if it saw me, I think.'

'Well, all right. But you haven't told me what to look for ...'

'When you see it, you'll know.'

I hesitated then. I began to get that eerie feeling again. What was it I was supposed to meet? And where would I meet it?

'Look,' I protested, 'you've got to give me some idea ...'

'Try the old kilns.'

'Well, all right. But you haven't told me what to look for ...'

'You'll know it when you see it. Aye.'

I looked along towards the old lime kilns. I even got my binoculars for a better look. But there was nothing stirring in that direction.

'I'll be waiting in the boathouse,' Joe said.

I still hesitated, looking ahead to the flat grass and the sea. For a second I thought maybe I shouldn't bother. I was under no obligation to go scouting around for some strange bird just because he said so. On the other hand, I didn't want to be called full of guilt or a coward or something.

I took a firm grip on my binoculars and started forward moving slowly and cautiously through the grass, and rounding the base of the rock. There was nothing there but the bleak land stretching on to the sea, and the sea birds and waders in flight. I began to get the feeling that he was having me on.

I paused for a moment, looking back over the harbour to where the ruins of the Priory stood out against the sky. A chill wind was coming in over the sea. Apart from the sound of the wind and the sea, and a few bird calls, the island was quiet. It was a strange place.

I shrugged the feeling away and started again towards the lime kilns. They were dug out of the rock the castle was on – deep high shafts going into the hillside. I approached cautiously, wondering which entrance to take. Then I thought I heard a sound from one kiln – a moaning sound. At first, I thought it was the sea, then I heard it again. I went towards that kiln, wondering whether it was a seal, in fact – maybe one that had been injured. Though why the old man should be so secretive about it, I couldn't tell. I remembered old legends, tales of terrible creatures like the Lambton Worm. That was daft, of course. I went on again, quietly, cautiously to the kilns and peered in. Nothing moved, but I had a weird sensation that something live was there. I went carefully inside, keeping close to the wall.

I stopped. Lying on the ground in one of the alcoves was a body, stretched out and covered with a blanket. Although it was gloomy in the kilns, I could make out the face clearly enough. It was Fordie Telford.

I was certain he was dead, he was so still and his face was so pallid. But then he moaned and stirred. 'Fordie!' I said urgently. His eyes opened and he looked at me. Then suddenly he was scrambling on his hands and knees – like an animal – farther into the kilns. 'Fordie!' I shouted again. 'It's me, Fordie – it's John!'

He was ill all right. He'd got very thin and he didn't seem to be able to stop shaking. And he looked wild and frightened and didn't know where he was. I think he knew who *I* was though. At least he didn't run from me again and he let me wrap the blanket round him. I tried to get out of him what had happened, but he just muttered to himself, something about the sea and the cold. And once he grasped my arm and exclaimed, 'Watch out for *him*!'

'Look, Fordie,' I said at last, 'you can't stay here. You'd

better come with me to Joe's cottage where you can get warm, and then I'll take you home. Your gran, you know, Fordie, she's been in a terrible state. Come on now.'

But he wouldn't come with me. Soon as I tried to get him out of the kilns, he was struggling and running in again.

Well it was a problem, so at last I wrapped the blanket round him again and told him I was going to have a talk to Joe and that I'd be back soon. I don't know whether he understood. He slumped down again, his eyes closed.

# 9

'It's Fordie Telford – it's Fordie Telford in the kilns – that's my pal that was lost with *Night Wind* . . .'

The old man sat there smoking his pipe, his face gnarled and brown like the trunk of an old tree. He was quite still, his silver eyes staring thoughtfully out of the open doorway of his boathouse towards the sea. He didn't seem to understand the importance of what I said. I was feeling so happy and excited that Fordie was alive after all, that I could have danced!

'That boy,' I repeated, 'he's Fordie Telford . . .'

'Aye. The migrant. What do you think of him, eh? There's one saved. That's a miracle, isn't it? The sea's given back one.'

'But how did he escape? He must have swam all that way . . .'

Joe nodded, and his gnarled hands made bumpy shapes in the air, 'Seal-like! Seal-like!'

I sat down. 'The creature you saw – the marks in the sand, the thing that rushed past me that night below the castle – that was Fordie! He's been on the island since Friday morning!' I could hardly believe it yet. And there was his gran ill with the shock, and the memorial service held for him, and all the time he was alive, on the island. 'We've got to get him home. We'll have to tell his gran. And you know he's ill? There's blankets and food in there with him – did you put them there? When did you find him? And why didn't you . . .?'

'Don't start assigning guilt, John Watt. Isn't a miracle enough for you without questioning it?'

A miracle, I thought scornfully, then I wondered. It was a bit of a miracle. After all, according to Andy Armstrong nobody had a chance when the coble went down. 'How can we get him home? He can't walk.'

He suddenly knocked the ashes out of his pipe. 'Now we'll just sit down and think. Make plans. That's what you always do, isn't it? Plans and notes and diagrams.'

'But Fordie's ill.'

'Aye, he's ill. Been ill a fair time now. A few more minutes isn't going to make any difference. I knew he was there the day I came to see you and you refused to come back with me to help . . .'

'But . . .'

'Refused! That's on your own conscience. He wasn't so ill then. Came out at nights and got water from the village pump and hunted round for food. Eggs he stole, and some bread went from one house that left a window open. Then he was ill and couldn't go out hunting. I did what I could for him when I found that out – but he was delirious then, off his head. Don't think he ever really knew who I was.'

I was puzzled. I couldn't understand why Fordie had hidden away like that. After all, he'd only to tell the islanders who he was and what had happened and they'd have had him back in no time. And then, the old man – why hadn't he got help sooner?

'There was no need to wait for me to come and help,' I objected. 'You could have asked anybody.'

Joe looked fiercely at me.

'Ever smelt fear on a man? I have. Always know fear when I'm near it – and that lad's frightened. Terrified. I know. That's what makes a fisherman different from the man next door – he knows what fear is. But there's fear and fear. Some's healthy, some's not. That's not. Fear and guilt. Fear and guilt.' He muttered on under his breath, and honestly I began to feel a bit creepy. I always expected he'd go off his head sometime. Then he glared at me. 'That's a problem for you to solve, John Watt. A burden to carry on your shoulders. What's he frightened of? And if you don't know why he's in hiding, do you dare to bring him out of hiding without his consent?'

I got the point all right. Fordie must have had some good reason for hiding out in the kilns, cold and hungry as he must have been. He hadn't even tried to get in touch with me. We couldn't risk bringing him out of hiding till we knew what it was all about. The old man wasn't all that daft, after all.

My excitement began to fade. I'd been envisaging phoning Jim Pollard the policeman with the news, and the look on old Mrs Telford's face when she was told, but now I saw those things couldn't be – not yet.

I looked steadily into his fierce, silver eyes, and he looked steadily into mine.

'Right?' he said.

'Right,' I said. 'But we have to get him somewhere warm and safe.'

'My cottage. But not till after dark.'

'Why after dark? We should take him now.'

'We canna risk being seen. We don't know whose gaze we're avoiding.'

I was a bit shaken by this new idea of his, but I supposed

he had a point. "All right,' I said. 'It'll be dark soon anyway.'

'Another quarter of an hour.' He seemed more peaceful and calm now. He was a strange man.

When it was dark we brought Fordie out of the kilns and took him to Joe's cottage. We didn't go through the village. We went round the harbour and over the Heugh, round the back of the village and through Joe's back garden. Nobody saw us.

Fordie staggered along with the two of us helping him. He seemed to know who I was by then, and he didn't show any fear of Joe – I suppose because Joe was with me. We put him to bed in the little attic bedroom and Joe packed hot-water bottles round him and gave him a hot drink. Fordie drank that greedily, then he murmured, 'Watch out for *him*,' and lay down and fell asleep. He looked very pale and tired in the candlelight. I was very worried about him.

'He should have a doctor to see him,' I said.

'He'll be all right. He'll be right as rain after a night's sleep and some solid food.'

I followed him downstairs and he started making tea.

'Well, I'm not so sure,' I said. 'We don't know how ill he is. He could die. Look, I can go out and phone a doctor – I could phone our doctor, and he could get over here straight away.' It was the sensible thing to do. Fordie looked so ill.

'Aye. And a doctor would have to fill in forms, and know names, and make reports, and everybody would know fast enough that the lad wasn't drowned.' He poured out the tea into two mugs and handed me one. 'And whoever he's frightened of would know as well.'

'Look,' I said, 'we don't *know* he's frightened. You're

only assuming he's frightened. And he might die just because you assumed he's frightened and won't get a doctor to him.'

'Assuming, am I?' His voice grew loud. 'Listen, John Watt, if he was in the *Night Wind*, and he swam ashore from her, he would know which ship capsized her, and who was responsible. Now if he wasn't afraid, he would have come straight out with that information, but he didn't. He hid himself.'

I looked into those silver-grey eyes. There was something hypnotic about him. I think I was half hypnotized by him then.

'And if he hid himself he was frightened of something back in that village of yours. Somebody he knew and who knew him.' He drank his tea noisily. The doubts I'd had were still there, but in the background. He was so certain he was right.

'You go about this thing carefully, John Watt. You could be in danger yourself if it got around that you were hunting somebody down.'

I found it hard to believe that one, but I didn't argue.

'Are you not going, John Watt?' the old man asked suddenly.

'Going? Well that's a change. You're usually asking why I don't stay.'

He stood up abruptly and began waving his arms about. 'Haven't you work to do? Isn't the task before you? What makes you such a procrastinator, John Watt?'

Well, I was fairly knocked over by that one. Me, a procrastinator? What was he on about?

'You must find out what's scaring him – you must find out, so that he can come out of hiding!' He sat down again, leaning forward and glaring at me. 'How will you begin?'

I couldn't meet his eyes. I didn't know how to begin. To find out about birds, you got yourself a good hiding-place from where you could watch them, and then you used your eyes and your time and patience. Here, I didn't even know what I was supposed to be watching, let alone finding a way of watching it. Still, I *would* watch and I *would* listen. I would do the best I could to solve the mystery and make it safe for Fordie to come home.

# 10

The island was just a dark smear on the horizon behind me. I felt a sudden fear of the place and a need to get away from it quickly, and I started to cycle fast back to Rudharbour. And from the road along the coast, I could catch glimpses now and then between the sand dunes and cliffs of the lights of the village, winking and friendly. I think it was those lights that pulled me up sharp. I stopped the bike and stood there in the darkness with the wind stirring among the sand and grasses. And it struck me like a bullet what I'd done. I'd left Fordie there on that bleak island that would soon be cut off again by the sea for hours, and nobody to look after him but a crazy old man. What if he was really ill and died? I kept on picturing Fordie as he'd lain in the kilns with his bruised face and his torn clothes, the blanket the old man had put over him thrown aside. Lying so still he might have been dead. And then in the candlelight in the bedroom with the grime washed from his face, but looking so pale, muttering occasionally and moving his head as though he were in pain.

Thinking over what could have happened to him and how ill he might be, I began to feel I'd been wrong in listening to Joe. Surely the thing to do was get Fordie a doctor and tell his gran he was safe? How could I face the old woman, knowing how she was grieving, and not tell her? Suppose Fordie died, just because he hadn't had medical attention? You're daft, John Watt, I told myself. Listening to a crazy old man like that. Pedalling grimly home I made up my mind that I could only allow myself that night and the next day, and if by that time, Wednesday night, I hadn't discovered anything to support the old man's ideas, then I'd go and see Jim Pollard and tell him everything. Smelling fear on a man, I thought derisively. I needed my brains examining believing a thing like that.

So I worked out a plan. From all accounts, some ship on that bit of coastline that night had cut the coble's nets and capsized her. Now whether or not it was something to do with that mystery ship that had made Fordie frightened – if he was frightened – it was as good a starting point as any for an inquiry. Which ship did it, and why didn't she look for survivors and report what had happened?

I had to get the details. I would have to find out what ships were in the area that night, and suddenly I remembered the map that had been drawn up and hung in the lifeboat station while the search for the coble was going on. Andy Armstrong had taken charge of it afterwards and it would be in the coastguard station now, I was sure.

I propped my bike up against the wall of our house, seeing the light shining through the curtains and wanting only to go inside and have something to eat and go to bed because I was hungry and dead tired. But I hadn't time to waste. I had to see that chart, and so I started to walk towards Sea Lonnen and Cross Point, but as I passed the lifeboat shed a match flared in the shadows. I went along quietly, leaning against the shed as I'd done the night Fordie went missing. I wished I knew the fishermen as well as Fordie did. They would let him into their conversations and talk to him like an equal. But I was always just

Fordie's friend, a stranger who knew nothing about their craft.

'What I say is you can't trust foreigners,' Alfie Hymas was saying. 'And you can't trust them to own up to what they've done. They won't have any investigations into what they were up to. You know that.'

'Nowt of the kind!' exclaimed Andy Armstrong.

'I'm telling you.'

'He's got a point.'

'Course I've got a point. Foreigners! Huh! Same as that young lad of the Watts – cheeky young pup standing around saying nothing and making you wonder what he's staring at, then coming flat out and telling you your own business! That's a foreigner all over.'

They say listeners hear no good of themselves. My face began to burn. I'd no idea that's what the villagers thought of me. For a few seconds I lost track of the conversation thinking about it – was I really like that?

'The Norwegians would have no good reason for not reporting what happened – if they were responsible. And whatever you say about John Watt, he was quite right about the Norwegian trawler – take the times she was passing, and she couldn't have cut the nets of the *Night Wind*, because the Hymases weren't fishing then.' That was Andy Armstrong.

'You were never very keen on sticking up for your own,' Alfie Hymas accused him, and that got Andy angry.

'Less of that, Alfie,' he said. 'You're no one to talk there. You're mighty keen all of a sudden to blame somebody for your brother's death, but you didn't speak to him much during the last six years, did you?'

'I had good reason – it was a matter of principle, as you

well know. My eldest son went down with the *Northumbrian Maid*.'

Alfie's voice was bitter, and the men murmured sympathetically, 'Aye, Alfie. Tragedy that was. He was a fine lad.'

'Taking that into account, Alfie, most of us were agreed about what the two Bobs did over the *Northumbrian Maid* – most of us agreed we'd have done the same. You were the only one came out calling them cowards,' said Andy.

'Now then, now then, Andy,' somebody said, 'we'll all be saying things we regret at this rate.'

'Not me,' said Andy. 'I never blamed the Hymases for what they couldn't help but do. Not me. And none of us knew what it was like to stand up and make that kind of accusation against a man who was well thought-of by the trawler owners and everybody else.'

'Well thought-of!' Alfie exclaimed scornfully. 'Well thought-of I don't think. It's not my way to speak ill of the dead but there's plenty would have backed up the two Bobs if they'd had the guts to come out and speak!'

'Ah well, it's all past history now. Best forgotten. Let it lie, Alfie. Does no good raking it up.'

There was a rather uncomfortable silence. What were they talking about, I wondered. I'd never known that Alfie Hymas didn't get on with the two Bobs. And what had happened over the *Northumbrian Maid* that made them fall out? That was the trawler lost in 1961 with Fordie's dad in her. It was a funny place, that village. If they didn't want you to know a thing, you didn't get to know it. People just didn't talk about it. They were close, as my dad would say.

Andy cleared his throat and had his last say, sternly,

'Well, you'd better watch what you're saying, all of you, about the Norwegians, because I'm telling you they weren't responsible.'

There was the tread of heavy feet as he left them. I waited a bit. The men didn't speak immediately. Then a voice said, 'He's mebbe right. We'd mebbes better wait for the results of the inquiry.'

It was like a red rag to a bull as far as Alfie was concerned. "*In*-quiry? *In*-quiry?' he demanded sarcastically. 'You expect the truth to come out at a *in*quiry? You must be barmy! What truth came out at the *Northumbrian Maid in*-quiry? You know as well as I do – they all got together and swore black's white the skipper was a fine lad, and had nowt on his conscience for what happened. And the result of that is he's strutting about today as if he *had* nowt on his conscience! If we wait for the *in*quiry the Norwegians'll be gone, and that'll be another injustice!'

He went on then about the Norwegians, and it didn't look as though I would hear any more about the *Northumbrian Maid*. And the light in the coastguard station up there on the point drew me towards it, tired though I was, so I left the shadow of the old shed and started up Sea Lonnen. Still, I thought as I went, there was some mystery about the *Northumbrian Maid* that would have to be looked into. After all, it was connected with Fordie because his dad and his cousin went down with the *Northumbrian Maid*, and it looked as though Alfie and the two Bobs had fallen out over that all those years ago.

Andy had a mug of tea beside him as he studied some papers. He looked up and didn't seem too pleased to see me.

'Now what do you want, John? You've no business here.'

I didn't say anything. I just stood where I could see the map they'd pinned up that showed the movements of shipping the night the coble had disappeared. I tried to memorize it in quick glances.

'Here, none of your silence with me. Speak up or get out.'

I suddenly remembered what the fishermen had said about me, and I flushed.

'Sorry,' I said. 'I just wondered whether there was anything new about the *Night Wind?*'

'There'll be nothing new till the inquiry. Now you get off home.'

'But you agree with me, it couldn't have been the Norwegians?'

'We'll wait for the inquiry. Is Mrs Telford pulling round?'

'She's a bit better, I think.'

'Aye. Well get yourself off home.'

For a minute, I stood there, thinking of the information I had that would have sent him racing for the police if I'd only told him!

'I warned you, lad, I won't have you staring at me and saying nowt!'

But I think the mystery of the *Night Wind* was troubling him as much as me, and instead of chasing me, he got up and came over to study the maps as well. We stood together, our eyes tracing the tracks of the ships that had passed along the Northumbrian coast early that Friday morning, and the light cast our shadows across the walls and the black stretches of window.

'See, there's the four cobles – they come out of Rudharbour half past nine, they go out about a mile and half and start fishing. Now, here's the *Night Wind*. Half past eleven – according to you – she lifts her nets and goes north ...'

'And she passes the Norwegian trawler coming south,' I put in.

'That's right. The Norwegian trawler passes her, cuts the *Pity Me's* nets, and goes to the North Shields. Meantime, the *Night Wind's* gone on north as far as the Inner Farne, and she casts her nets and starts fishing again – probably about midnight. Now what happened next?' Andy Armstrong rubbed his hand across his face. 'She wasn't there at dawn. There were ships passing then, and they none of them saw her. Now, this dotted line, that's the track of the trawler *Mayflower*, coming out of North Shields and passing the Farnes about twelve thirty. This is the track of the *Reginald*, another trawler, coming south into North Shields and passing the Farnes about four in the morning.'

'Did they see the coble?'

'The *Reginald* saw no sign of a coble near the Farnes. And the *Mayflower* should be in to Rudharbour tomorrow with the herring, and she'll maybe have some news.'

Andy Armstrong began pacing up and down the small hut, his footsteps echoing on the floor, his shadow trailing him, big and reluctant, across the chart.

He stopped suddenly, his head on one side. We'd both heard it – footsteps climbing the stairs to the hut. There was a tap at the door and Will Martin came in. He stood with his hands pushed into the pockets of his navy raincoat, looking at us steadily from under his brows.

'Evenin', Andy.'

'Evenin', Will.' There was a touch of frost in Andy's tone, I thought, but nothing like the enmity of the fishermen to Will Martin. Will Martin nodded at me, a curt seaman kind of nod, and I was quite confused by that attention from him.

'Sorry about the *Night Wind*.'

'Aye. It's a tragedy. Mystery as well. I was just trying to sort over the facts. You see, this is the chart of the area for that night . . .'

They seemed to fill the hut, those two men, and I was squashed beside the wall near the map.

'I was in that area myself, of course, that Friday morning,' said Will Martin.

'Aye. This is the track of the *Jenny Mary* – you left North Shields and came north, passing the *Pity Me* about one in the morning – so we've been told.'

'That's right. She signalled me to pass on the side away from the nets, and I did that.'

'You were on the bridge yourself?'

'I always am, leaving port.'

'Well, you must have been by the Farnes about half past one?'

'About then.'

'Did you have any sight of the coble?'

Will Martin hesitated just a second as though he were thinking. I looked up into his face, and he looked into mine, but not seeing me because his thoughts were elsewhere.

'Didn't see her,' he said at last, 'but that's not to say she wasn't there. She could have been farther inshore.'

Andy sighed. 'Aye, it's a mystery. If there'd been a heavy sea even – but a night as calm as that – it just doesn't make sense.'

'It must have been a passing ship cut her nets and

swamped her, mustn't it?' I asked. 'There's no other explanation, is there?'

Will Martin looked sharply at me.

'Still on about that, are you?'

'That's the tale that's going about the village,' Andy put in quickly. 'You've no call to be repeating it, lad. Especially since you know nothing about such things. If that had happened, the ship responsible would have put out a call for help.'

'I've heard they don't report cutting a coble's nets.'

'Cutting nets is one thing, swamping a boat's another.'

'But things aren't always that simple, are they? I mean, things don't get reported always, do they? Wasn't there some doubt about what happened with the *Northumbrian Maid*, for example?'

If I'd threatened them both with a gun, they couldn't have been more tense. I could feel it, tangible, in the air around us. They both looked at me, and then quickly at each other and away. Then Will Martin fixed his gaze on me, and Andy looked uncomfortable, clearing his throat nervously and rubbing his hand over his face. Then he exploded. 'You daft young blighter! What you on about? What you saying a thing like that for?' he shouted, and I sort of took a step back from him, I was so astonished.

'N-nothing – no reason,' I stammered.

'Well don't make such daft comments.'

'Now then, Andy, don't upset the lad.' Will Martin's voice was as cold and calm as his eyes. 'He maybe had some reason for saying that. Did you, lad?'

Between Andy's anger and Will Martin's icy calmness – well, I've never felt so uncomfortable. 'I just thought – I'd just heard – well the two Bobs were connected with both ships, and didn't they fall out with Alfie Hymas over the *Northumbrian Maid*? It was that made me think of her.'

There was a sudden releasing of the tension. Andy sat down at the table, looking over his papers again, and Will Martin turned to the chart.

'That all? Listening to old gossip – forget it, lad. There's no connection there.'

I was glad to slip out and leave them talking. They didn't seem to notice me going. There was something strange about the *Northumbrian Maid*, that was certain. There was something nobody wanted to talk about.

At home my dad was sitting in front of the fire and only the firelight was lighting the room.

'By, lad,' he said to me, 'you're keeping some late hours, our John. It'll have to stop, you know.' His voice was kind.

'They were talking about the coble. Along at the shed. Alfie Hymas.' I suddenly felt so tired I could hardly speak. I dropped into a chair and felt the warmth of the room spread through me.

'Are you not hungry? You've been out for hours and had no dinner.'

There were some pasties and sausage rolls that mam had made. I had a cup of cocoa with them, sitting in front of the fire. It was difficult to keep awake.

'Dad,' I said, 'you know about the Hymas's coble? Well somebody must have been responsible, mustn't they? Why do you think they haven't come out and said so? I mean, it must have been an accident – so why keep quiet about it?'

'Plenty of reasons. Thing like that might lose a man his job – and he wouldn't get another easy. Better to live with it than have everybody know about it and point you out and talk about you.'

'They still think it was the Norwegians.'

'Aye. Well, maybe it was. Your mam's in the front room sitting with old Mrs Telford. The poor soul's been taken bad again. Effect of the memorial service, I expect.'

That took my thoughts straight back to Fordie. He should have been brought home, I thought, and I got so desperate just then that I almost blurted the whole story out to my dad. To stop myself I said good night and went up to the attic. Anyway, I could work things out better there.

First of all I drew the map I'd seen at the coastguard station into the back of my field notebook. There were quite a number of ships in the area that night, after all, but it wasn't easy to pinpoint one that might have been responsible for the *Night Wind*'s wrecking. It looked as though she disappeared between midnight and four in the morning, and the only ships in the area then were the *Mayflower* and the *Jenny Mary* that both passed the Farnes, and the other three cobles that were fishing off Rudharbour until four in the morning when I'd seen their lights from the point. Could one of those five ships have swamped the *Night Wind*?

Holy Island Joe thought that Fordie was afraid of someone in the village, someone he knew there who had been responsible for wrecking the coble. If that was true then, apart from the three cobles, the *Jenny Mary* was the only other ship in the area that had connections with Rudharbour through her master, Will Martin. I didn't know about the *Mayflower*, but she should be in harbour soon and then I could find out. But it did mean that somebody in Rudharbour knew more than he was saying. Tomorrow I would watch them all, carefully and all the time. I would note down what they all said and did in a field notebook. Somebody was sure to give himself away if I watched carefully enough.

It was then I fell asleep with my head on the desk, and it must have been an hour later when the sound of my mam and dad coming upstairs to bed wakened me. I got up, yawning, to stagger off to bed, when something came back to me. It was something I'd seen that Friday morning early on the point. That was it! The lights of the cobles fishing off Rudharbour. The lights of *two* cobles. But there should have been *three*!

# 11

It was the haven-screamers woke me next morning. Half past five it was, a sunny morning with a nip in the air, and the screeching of gulls was deafening. There was a floating, shrieking umbrella of them over a small trawler that had just moored in the harbour. I could see the name on her bows – the *Mayflower*. A lorry from the herring curing-shed was drawn up alongside her, and they were preparing to unload her catch. I got ready and took a new notebook and pencil and went out on to the harbour. I chose my place carefully, climbing up on the harbour wall where I could see the whole of the village in a panorama in front of me.

I didn't feel happy about what I was going to do. In fact I felt very nervous. Knowing what people in that village thought of me already, I couldn't see that it would increase my popularity if I sat on the harbour wall all day watching them. There was no telling how they might react to that. And then, whoever was the guilty one in the village would have me there as a target – a sitting duck, all right! But I thought of Fordie lying sick in the old man's cottage. He could be a lot worse now and I wouldn't know. I had to get some information out of that village before nightfall.

They had lifted the hatches of the *Mayflower* and were bringing the herring up in baskets, swinging them by a crane on to the lorry where they were loaded into boxes.

The haven-screamers went frantic. They swooped down and pinched fish from the baskets, they swallowed fish whole, they tore fish apart in squabbling groups, and they perched uneasily on the trawlers and the roofs of the shed, anxiously watching the silver catch being carted out of their reach. Now and then an angry fisherman would wave his arms and shout at them, like I'd seen Joe do, but it didn't stop them.

The skipper of the *Mayflower* stood on the harbourside smoking a cigarette. Two of the crew were helping unload, and a boy in a blue woollen cap sat on the ship's rail, rising and falling with the movement of the ship as if he'd grown there. They were all strangers to me. Smoke rose from the chimneys of the cottages behind. Our chimney had been going for a while, then Alfie Hymas's started up. The Telfords' house showed no life.

It was half past six when the *Sea Witch* came in. Alfie Hymas had brought in herring, and although his catch couldn't measure up to the *Mayflower*'s he was obviously steamed up because she'd got in before him. He started ordering his son around, and the two of them began unloading boxes of fish. The haven-screamers swirled over to them, dividing their attention between the two ships.

By eight o'clock, the *Mayflower*'s catch was unloaded, and the boy sitting on her rails leapt down and started to clean her decks. He whistled shrilly all the time, and now and then exchanged a word or two at the top of his voice with the men packing the *Sea Witch*'s catch on to the lorry. There was something familiar about that boy. By that time as well, the other cobles were in harbour, and Alfie Hymas, as soon as he'd settled up about his catch, went round to them and started haranguing the other fisherman. I couldn't hear what he was talking about, but I would have bet it was the Norwegians. Alfie Hymas, I noted, who had lost a son in the *Northumbrian Maid*, and had never forgiven his brother and cousin for refusing to speak up against her skipper at the inquiry. Alfie Hymas who was out fishing the night the *Night Wind* was lost, and who was now doing his best to lay the blame on the Norwegian trawler in spite of any evidence you gave him that she wasn't responsible. Could he have a reason for wanting to put the blame on somebody else?

About half past eight, the boy from the *Mayflower* took off his oilskin coat, rolled up the sleeves of his sweater, lit a cigarette and started to stroll round the harbour to where I was sitting. He stopped beside me.

'It's What John Watt, isn't it?' he asked cheekily.

'Charlie Barley!' That's what we used to call him. I recognized him now – Charlie Milburn who was in the junior school when I was there five or six years ago. He'd been one of the worst for teasing me, and I'd never been able to get my own back because he'd been a few years older and always bigger and stronger. He'd been a good friend of Fordie's though. He got up on the wall beside me.

'What you doing, kiddar?'

'Making notes. On the birds.'

He drew on his cigarette.

'Go on.'

'I am.'

'What for?'

'I'm interested.'

'Barmy!' Anything to do with paper and ink had always earned his deepest scorn, I remembered.

Over at the other side of the harbour two men stood,

apart from each other but both watching Charlie and me. One was Alfie Hymas and the other was Will Martin. I hadn't seen him come down from Sea Lonnen. Alfie Hymas turned away when he saw me looking at him. Will Martin went on smoking his pipe and watching us. Then he went over to speak to the *Mayflower*'s skipper. Will Martin, I thought, who was called the crack skipper but was really master of a very small steamer that made regular and monotonous trips out of Shields, north to Scotland and back. Will Martin who hadn't seen any coble by the Farnes at one o'clock that Friday morning. Will Martin who kept himself to himself and wasn't liked in Rudharbour.

'Heard about the loss of the coble?' I asked Charlie.

'Why, aye. Heard it over the radio when we were fishing. Mystery that is. The two Bobs knew these waters like the backs of their hands. We passed the *Night Wind*, you know. Friday morning, it was, about half past twelve. She was all right then.'

'Did you see her?'

'Oh aye. It was a calm night, good visibility. Why man, she signalled us to keep clear of her nets. I was on deck and I hailed Tanner Hymas – good pal of my dad's Tanner was, you see.'

That seeemed to clear the *Mayflower*. Charlie Milburn wasn't a lad who would tell a lie.

'Who's the nut-case?'

'What nut-case?'

'Owner of the *Sea Witch*. He's never stopped talking since he got in. Alfie Hymas, is it?'

'Yes.'

'Still living here, are you? Don't know how you stick it. At the grammar school, I bet? By, you must be nuts. I'm a deckie-learner on the *Mayflower*. You should get yourself a job on a ship, kiddar. It's a man's life. Not sitting around writing about birds! That's cissy!'

He threw the remains of his cigarette into the harbour.

'Fordie Telford around the day?'

'Fordie?' His question gave me such a shock that for a second I thought he must know Fordie was still alive. 'What d'you mean?'

'Fordie Telford – you know, Fordie. He was my pal at school.'

'Did you not hear?'

'What?'

'Fordie was in the coble. He went down with her.'

Charlie's face paled underneath his fisherman's tan.

'You're kiddin'.'

I shook my head. I didn't like giving him a shock like that when I knew Fordie was alive. But I couldn't tell him the truth.

Charlie got down from the wall and started walking along the harbour. He stopped with his back to me, and stood looking out to sea. After a few minutes he lit another cigarette and came back. He didn't look at me.

'By, I didn't know. I thought it was just the two Bobs. Poor lad. By, I bet his gran's upset.'

'She's been in hospital.'

'You know, the last time I saw Fordie he was down at Shields. Said he was looking for a job. Always wanted to go to sea did Fordie. I was going to help him, but I hadn't the time. I was off on a trip. If he'd got a job then he wouldn't have been in that coble . . .'

Fordie was often down at Shields, I knew. But I always thought he went to fish and look at the ships. I didn't know he'd been after a job. After all, he would have another year at school yet.

'Did you not see Fordie in the coble that night?'

'Don't be so daft! How much do you think you can see out there at midnight?' He thought for a moment. 'Funny thing he didn't hail me, but. He must have known it was me talking to Tanner.'

Somebody from the deck of the *Mayflower* stood up and yelled at Charlie, 'You, yer young blighter, come on! You're keeping us all back!'

Charlie cast a belligerent look in that direction, and pulled his cap farther down over his ears. 'I'd better be getting on. See you.' He walked away, a lot less cockily than when he came. I watched him go thinking that I must tell him as soon as I could that Fordie was safe.

He joined the crew of the *Mayflower* and they strolled away towards Ridley's corner. There was a small café round that way and they were off to have some breakfast no doubt. I was getting hungry myself.

Alfie Hymas and his son walked away along the harbour to their cottage. Going for breakfast as well. Will Martin went after them towards Ridley's corner. Going for his car, I supposed.

'Our John!' It was my mam yelling across to me. 'Breakfast!'

'I don't want any breakfast, mam,' I said when I got home. It cost me a lot to say that because I was hungry.

'Go on. You can't go to school on an empty stomach! And you'll miss that bus!'

'I feel sick.'

'Sick?' She looked closely at me. 'You look all right. Have you been sick?'

'It'll be all the trouble over Fordie upsetting him,' said Mrs Telford. 'Let the lad have a day off school and get over it.'

'He was off yesterday.'

'Won't do him any harm.'

'Well, I don't know . . .'

So I had old Mrs Telford to thank for that day off school. And I had myself to thank for not getting any breakfast. Being sick I couldn't very well eat. I managed to grab an apple, though, before I went out again. The lorry had gone, back to the curing station, and the fires were going up there and the smell of the burning of oak chippings that they used to smoke the herrings drifted down to the harbour. The cobles were moored and deserted. There were visitors sitting and strolling about and walking up to the cross on the point. Along at Ridley's corner, Will Martin was cleaning his car. Andy Armstrong was leaning on the harbour wall and looking across at me scribbling.

I wondered when Charlie had last seen Fordie at Shields. Might be a good idea to find out. And then I had to find out about the cobles that night . . .

Andy Armstrong came out along the harbour towards me. Andy Armstrong who'd been skipper of a trawler sailing out of Shields for years and was now retired and a coastguard. And a local man as well, who'd been born in Rudharbour, and knew everything and everybody about the place. A man who stuck to the rules and tried to be fair-minded.

'What you up to, lad? What on earth are you scribbling in that book?'

'I'm just observing.'

He grunted.

'Not going to school?'

'I've been a bit sick.'

'You were having a word with the deckie-learner off the *Mayflower?*'

'Charlie Milburn. He was at school with me.'

'No doubt you were asking questions about the *Night Wind?* What did he tell you?'

'He said they saw her, and he hailed Tanner Hymas.'

'That all?'

'I think I've got another lead.'

'I wish you would give up thinking, lad, and we might all have a bit of peace.'

'Last Friday morning, I was up early on the point bird-watching.'

He grunted again.

'I could see the lights of the cobles fishing off Rud-harbour.'

'Nothing new in that.'

'But, Mr Armstrong, there were only two cobles – not three.'

'Are you sure?'

'Dead certain.'

Old Mrs Telford came out of our house and went in next door. I saw the blinds being pulled up in the front room. She'd said she would go in that day and get the fire going. A group of fishermen was gathering on the harbour. Must have had their breakfasts. Alfie Hymas joined them. I could hear Alfie's voice clear across the harbour, though I couldn't make out what he was saying. A net was got out and stret-ched over the sand while a tear in it was mended. The gulls seemed to think that was a good sign and came whirling and plunging about the harbour again.

'I'd best go and ask about that while the coble owners are around,' Andy Armstrong said.

I saw him approach the group of fishermen, and I could see they were listening to him. Then there was some talking, and Alfie Hymas seemed to be explaining. Andy looked across at me, and so did Alfie Hymas. Then the talk went on again. I wondered what had been said. For a few minutes, I thought I was going to find out. Alfie Hymas left the other men and started walking fast and angry round the harbour towards me. I bent over my book and pretended not to see him. The minutes went by, but he didn't arrive. At last I looked up. He must have changed his mind. He was walking back again.

I saw Mrs Telford come out of her cottage. She stood a few minutes looking across at us. The crew of the *Mayflower* came round Ridley's corner. They were walking slowly and as if they'd enjoyed their breakfasts. Charlie walked behind them by himself. He saw Mrs Telford standing at our front door and went over and spoke to her. Then he went to his ship and she went inside. The harbour was busy, and some of the caravaners were down buying fish. The seagulls were still there, but quieter now, perched on the cottage roofs and digesting the fish they'd stolen. Half a dozen gulls settled on the water, floating comfortably as they preened and chattered like old women.

It was when I saw the *Mayflower* casting her moorings and preparing to leave harbour that I had a sudden thought. As the trawler passed me with Charlie waving from her deck I shouted to him.

'Charlie!'

'Ay!'

'When did you last see Fordie?'

'Told you! Down Shields!'

'But *when?*'

The *Mayflower* was past me now, with Charlie deep in thought. I didn't think he'd remember. Then he turned. His voice was dwindling as the ship left harbour.

'Kiddar!'

'Yes?'

'Last – Thursday – night – before we left for the fishing!'

The *Mayflower* sailed between the harbour's piers, bucking and lurching as she reached the open sea. She disappeared behind the headland as she moved south.

He must be wrong, I thought. It couldn't have been last Thursday night he saw Fordie at Shields, because Fordie was in the coble. Then I thought again. If Charlie had been hurrying off on his last trip it was something he wouldn't get mixed up about, and if Charlie was right that meant Fordie Telford hadn't been in the coble. If he'd been down at Shields he couldn't have been. He'd been looking for a job. I'd been right from the start. He'd been running away. So that meant – that meant there were *two* mysteries. Who swamped the coble, and what did Fordie Telford do that night before he swam ashore to the island?

'You were right, lad.' It was Andy Armstrong again. 'About the cobles. One of them followed the *Night Wind* north about midnight.'

'It was Alfie Hymas in the *Sea Witch*.'

'How did you know that?'

'I guessed.'

'Well, it beats me. But it's nothing to make a fuss over. The *Sea Witch* didn't go far north – not as far as the Farnes.'

That would be Alfie's story, I thought.

'Mr Armstrong. I've found out something about Fordie.'

'Now, look, lad . . .'

'But it's important, Mr Armstrong. Charlie Milburn says he saw Fordie last Thursday night late, down at Shields.'

Andy Armstrong said nothing.

'You see, Mr Armstrong, that means he wasn't in the coble.'

'I can see what it means.' And after a bit, 'I don't set a lot of store by anything a lad like that deckie-learner has to say.'

'But he was a pal of Fordie's . . .'

'He could be wrong about the day he saw the lad. So give it up. I don't want you upsetting Mrs Telford again.'

'There's just one thing,' I said.

'What?'

'If he *did* see Fordie that night, Fordie must be alive still.'

'I'm not daft. I can see that.' He stood rubbing his hand over his face. He was disturbed was Andy Armstrong. 'Better have something done about this. Pollard better be told.'

'Told what, Andy?' Will Martin had come up quietly behind us. His hands were wet from washing down his car and he was drying them on a rag.

'Mr Martin, I was talking to the deckie-learner on the *Mayflower* and he told me . . .'

'Aye, I saw you talking.'

'He told me Fordie Telford was down at Shields last Thursday.'

I thought he would say something, but he didn't.

'You see what that means? It means he wasn't in the coble.'

'Where is he then?'

He turned and looked hard at me. I shook my head. I couldn't give even Will Martin that last piece of information.

'Jim Pollard had better be told about this,' said Andy Armstrong.

'Wait a bit, Andy.' Will Martin laid a hand on his arm. 'A deckie-learner on a trawler's not a very reliable kind of witness. We'll look fools if we stir things up for no good reason. We'd better look into this ourselves a bit first. What d'you think?'

'Aye, well. You could be right. It looks as if I'll have to go down to Shields anyway to stop that lot of ninnies making fools of themselves.' He walked off again towards the fishermen.

'Not at school, John?'

'Haven't been well.'

Will Martin stood looking back at the village.

'You've got a good view here. What are you up to?'

'Finding out about people. You have to watch them to find out about them.'

His profile was sharp against the sky, a narrow head with a lean nose and a short stern upper lip and jutting jaw. There was a deep line between his eyebrows and it seemed to me the face of a man who had had a lot of hard thoughts to think and decisions to make that had moulded those lines. His skin was the colour of mooring ropes that had been soaked again and again, and dried again and again in the wind and the sun till they were a sort of greyish sandy colour, and his eyes were a deep brown.

He looked at me quickly.

'You'll know me next time, John,' he said, and I flushed, realizing I'd been staring again. I couldn't help it though.

You're supposed to be able to read a person's character from his face. And to read anything, you had to look at it.

'There's Alfie Hymas trying to persuade them to go down to Shields and beat up the Norwegians for swamping the coble. You'd better make a note of that, lad.' He was sharp was Will Martin. 'Are you on the same track as Alfie?'

'Alfie's on the wrong track. And he maybe knows it.'

'That's very subtle, John.'

The fishermen suddenly moved off in a crowd towards Ridley's corner, leaving Andy Armstrong staring after them. Then Andy shouted 'Hi, Alfie! Hang on a minute!' and he followed them. In a few minutes we heard the sound of their cars starting up.

'They'll be off after the Norwegians,' said Will Martin.

'Mr Martin,' I said, 'was Andy Armstrong skipper of the *Northumbrian Maid*?'

'Don't be stupid!' he snapped and walked away quickly to Ridley's corner. I heard his car a bit later as he drove out of the village.

The people from the caravan site started walking up to The Rud – and their dinners, I supposed. A couple of fishermen's wives went with their shopping baskets towards Ridley's. Three or four gulls swooped across the harbour, calling disconsolately. The village was quiet now. I thought I'd better have my dinner. I thought I'd put one or two things into motion.

Just the same, I felt a bit nervous walking alone towards the cottages. Suppose the old man was right and somebody decided I was dangerous? I wasn't sure yet that I knew whom I had to guard against.

# 12

'How you feeling now, our John?'

'Not so bad, Mam.'

'Fresh air'll have done him good,' my dad said. 'Now let's see you eat a good dinner.'

'I think he's been having us on,' said my mam. 'Not much wrong with him.'

I had sat down on the sofa beside old Mrs Telford, but I saw something then that had me jumping up again.

'What's this?'

Propped up on the mantelpiece against the blue china vase that I had bought my mam for her birthday last year was a photograph, a photograph of a trawler with the name *Northumbrian Maid* on her bows and a man and a boy standing on the quay beside her. The boy looked so like Fordie Telford it wasn't true.

'It's Mrs Telford's, our John, so leave it alone now,' said my mam.

'It's George's dad and his cousin,' said old Mrs Telford. 'And that's the ship they was lost in, the *Northumbrian Maid*. I like to keep it by me. And I've one of George here in me handbag. It's all I have left of them.' She put a handkerchief to her eyes, but she didn't cry now.

'The *Northumbrian Maid*,' I said, 'that was the trawler the two Hymases sailed in, wasn't it?'

'The two Bobs, aye. Not Alfie Hymas. The Bobs sailed in her and my lad and my daughter's lad, and Alfie Hymas's eldest son. They used to call her *The Rudharbour Ferry* at Shields, there was so many Rudharbour men in her crew. That was just joking, of course. She turned out an unlucky ship in the end. There was only her skipper and the two Bobs was saved after she went down.'

'How was she lost, Mrs Telford?'

'Now, our John, give over pestering Mrs Telford with questions.'

'No, no. He's not pestering. She was lost off Iceland in that bad winter of 1961. The storms finished her. She was an old ship, you see, but all right while the weather lasted, my lad used to say.'

'Was there something – I mean, was there some mystery about the way she was lost?'

'Well, there was some talk at first from the two Bobs that it was all her skipper's fault. They said he'd taken one risk too many and he should have made for port as soon as the weather worsened and not gone on fishing. But then, you know, it was their word against the skipper's, and he was a good skipper and well thought-of. So they didn't go on with it. There was some in the village thought they were wrong, but I always considered they knew best what they were up to. When a thing's done, it's done, and might as well be let to lie. And if it was the skipper's fault, I always think he would suffer enough having the loss of those men on his conscience. Aye, it mightn't show in his face, but it must show in his heart.'

So that was why Alfie quarrelled with the two Bobs. He would think they should have spoken up at the inquiry into the loss of the *Northumbrian Maid*. And his enmity continued all those years. That was strange, I thought. But Alfie was a fiery man. I could well see him cutting the nets of the *Night Wind* just intending to give the two Bobs a bit of trouble. Then, when he found he'd swamped her by accident, coming back to Rudharbour and saying nothing and trying to put the blame on the Norwegian trawler. It seemed to me it all fitted. And it seemed to me that Alfie Hymas was the one Fordie had to be afraid of. The only question to answer now was how Fordie got mixed up in the business of the *Night Wind*.

And there was something else as well.

'Mrs. Telford,' I asked, 'who was the skipper of the *Northumbrian Maid?*'

Mrs Telford gave me a sharp look, then she turned away, shaking her head. 'That's no business of a lad like you. That's in the past, and it should stay there. I'm not one to keep a thing up against anybody.'

'Come now, our John. Stop *pestering* Mrs Telford. The dinner's ready. Come on now, sit up.'

I might have known I'd find nothing out in that village.

'Alfie Hymas and the fishermen have gone down to Shields to beat the Norwegians up,' I said. 'They think the Norwegian trawler swamped the coble.'

'Alfie Hymas should mind his own business,' said Mrs Telford sharply. 'He would have been better if he'd made his peace with the two Bobs before they were lost.'

I went out again after dinner, and I felt more nervous than ever because I had a feeling things would start moving. But I had to go out, and had to stay near the Harbour Road this time. I had to be in the middle of things.

Mrs Telford and my mam came out together and went along to Ridley's. Then my dad came across to me.

'What you up to, our John? Sitting about here writing – what you doing?'

'Studying the birds ...'

'Well, I don't know. You've sat here the livelong day. I hope you're getting something out of it ...'

He went off in the direction of The Rud.

The visitors wandered aimlessly about. A little group of them collected near the blackboard one of the fishermen had set up by the harbour saying:

TRIPS TO THE FARNES
3 p.m.
6/- ADULTS
3/- CHILDREN

About three I heard the cars coming back, roaring down the hill into the village. The fisherman who ran trips to the Farnes in his coble came stotting along the harbour with the beginnings of a black eye. In spite of that, he and his crew began herding people into his coble, and not very pleasantly. The coble's engine roared and the boatload went out of the harbour. More of the men came back along to their cottages looking subdued. It mustn't have been a successful fight, and Alfie couldn't be very popular, I thought.

It wasn't long after that Andy Armstrong drove along and he stopped beside me, opening the car window.

'Still here, lad? Got nothing better to do?'

'Did they fight the Norwegians?' I asked.

'Oh aye. They had a right bust up. Didn't do any good and they got the worst of it. Look, lad, I had a word with that fellow – the deckie-learner – before I left Shields.'

'He told you about Fordie?'

'He did not. Said he'd seen nothing. Took it all back.

Now I don't know who's having who on, but you'd better stop it, John Watt, before it ends in trouble.'

That's a bit queer, I thought. In fact, that was very queer. A few hours ago Charlie Milburn tells me he saw Fordie at Shields last Thursday night, and a few hours later he tells Andy Armstrong it wasn't true and he didn't see Fordie. That wasn't like Charlie Milburn. Especially if a pal was concerned, Charlie Milburn wouldn't let you down. What was the matter with him? I felt really vexed with him, I can tell you. You can't have people messing about with evidence that way. How was I going to make out a case if he kept changing his mind? And now I couldn't get hold of him to ask what he thought he was playing at.

There was Will Martin coming back now, walking past me on the other side of the Harbour Road, not looking in my direction, looking straight ahead, frowning. Not really like Will Martin to look worried about something. He didn't see me at all. He walked straight past me on to Sea Lonnen.

A motor bike came along the street and stopped beside me. The fellow on the bike was just a few years older than me. He came across.

'I'm looking for a fellow called Watt. D'you know where I'll find him?'

'I'm John Watt.'

'Well, that's a bit of luck. Charlie Milburn sent me. Sent a message for you. Said he wouldn't come here himself for all the tea in China.'

'What's happened to Charlie?'

'Nothing yet. But he's frightened of what will happen. It's something about somebody called Fordie, I think he said.'

'That's right.'

'Well, he says what he said about Fordie's wiped out, see? He never saw him at Shields. Charlie got a message passed to him to forget all about it, see? Otherwise he'd be carved up. Well, Charlie says it's not worth all that much to him, and you'd better watch out for yourself. Got it?'

I got it all right. That's why Charlie went back on what he said. Somebody getting at him. Somebody wanting to hush things up. Must have frightened Charlie all right. But who had frightened him? Nearly every man in the village had been down at Shields that afternoon. Alfie Hymas among them. I was sure it was Alfie Hymas. I was certain of it. He had the motive and he had the opportunity, and his behaviour since then all pointed to a guilty man trying to protect himself.

And Fordie was linked up with it all right. Alfie wouldn't have tried to silence Charlie if Fordie hadn't been linked up with it. Fordie must know. I hadn't worked out yet how he knew, but he must know. He must know Alfie had a hand in sinking the *Night Wind*.

The coble came in from the Farnes just as my dad came back home. He stopped to watch the passengers disembark and drift away about the village. He took a look at me, still wondering what I was up to. Then he went into our house.

It was just then that Alfie Hymas drove along the Harbour Road to the old shed, parked his car, and came straight back to me.

'Look lad!' he shouted. 'I've had just about enough of you! What've you been saying to Andy Armstrong about me? Eh? What've you been suggesting?'

His face was very red and angry, thrust into mine.

'I haven't said anything. I only asked if one of the cobles ...'

'Don't give me those lies!' His hand came down stingingly on my face and I overbalanced and fell off the wall. I crouched there.

'Now then, Alfie, what's all this?'

It was Jim Pollard, the policeman. I was glad to see him. He helped me up and I could feel my legs trembling.

'He hit me,' I said.

'Aye. I saw that. You can't go knocking people about like that, Alfie.'

'Look. I'm fed up with this kid. He's trying to blacken my reputation. You know what he's up to? He's trying to make out I murdered my own brother. *That*'s what he's doing. And you're the one should be stopping him!'

'Come on now, Alfie. I can hardly believe that.'

'He's been telling Andy Armstrong that I followed the *Night Wind* north that night she was lost and that I deliberately swamped her. That's what he's hinting at. And I'll tell you something else. He's trying to put it about that the Telford lad's still alive. Now either that lad's off his head or he's just plain bad and either way he should be locked up!'

The way he put it gave me a shock. It made what I was trying to do seem terribly wrong, and all I was trying to do was help Fordie.

'Mr Pollard,' I said, 'it's not true – not really.'

'Have you been asking questions again about the coble? And are you still trying to prove the Telford lad ran away that night?' the policeman asked me sternly.

I couldn't really deny that. I didn't say anything.

'Now listen to me, John Watt. I won't give you another warning. I don't know what's got into you, because you weren't a bad lad once, and you come of respectable parents. But if I hear one more complaint about you in this matter, I'll be paying you a visit. Understand?'

I nodded.

'Right then. Now, Alfie, you heard what I said. Leave the boy alone and let me attend to the matter.'

My mam had just got back home and she saw me with the policeman. She stopped at our door and shouted across, 'You all right, our John?' her voice full of meaning, threatening that if the policeman was bothering me she would come across soon enough and bother him. I said I was all right. 'Your tea'll be ready in ten minutes then!'

Alfie Hymas went away to the fishermen. As they went about stowing nets into the cobles I could see them talking and I got some black looks. The fishermen would stick together, and turn against me, I knew that. The policeman walked slowly away towards Ridley's corner.

My face burned where Alfie Hymas had hit me. I scowled across at him and the fishermen, but really I was very frightened. The evening was growing cooler and the shadows longer as the sun sank behind the Cheviots, and as the village darkened I began to panic. I knew where the danger lay for Fordie – and me – now. It was Alfie Hymas that had to be watched. But Fordie was miles away on the island that would be cut off by the tide again in a few hours, and I was in Rudharbour with no means of getting Fordie off the island quickly. Come to that, would I dare walk through the village after dark, knowing Alfie Hymas was probably looking out for me?

But I had to do it. I had to get Fordie off that island, that evening if possible, and take him straight to Pollard's house. Once Jim Pollard saw Fordie was alive he would listen to my story of how the coble was swamped. Alfie

Hymas might be able to pull the wool over everybody's eyes now, but I held the winning card. I had Fordie, and I knew the truth, and I wouldn't give up till it was known.

I crossed the Harbour Road to our house and just then the light was switched on in the living-room and there was everything looking peaceful and normal. My mam was sitting on the couch. But behind me I knew there was Alfie Hymas watching.

I was glad to get into the house, where I felt safe. My dad had just had his bath in preparation for his medical the next day. We hadn't a bathroom, so we had to have baths in the kitchen, and he was just coming out, rubbing his head with a towel, as I came in.

'Well,' he said, 'how do I look with the dirt off? By, our John, what's the matter? You look as if you've seen a ghost.'

'It's all this sitting on cold stone walls,' said my mam. 'It's given him a chill on the stomach. It's bed for you after tea, lad.'

# 13

I dare say I did look as if I'd seen a ghost. I know I was feeling very shaky as I sat down.

'Are you not well, our John? Get the lad a drink of water.'

'I'm all right. Honest.'

'You look it! Here. Have a sup of this.'

They stood looking at me while I drank the water. I said I would be all right just lying on the couch by the fire, so they let me stay for a bit. I felt as though I wanted to have people round me and not to be alone upstairs. And I wanted to think of what I was going to do. How was I to get Fordie off the island? He couldn't walk far, and I couldn't see how I could get an ambulance over there. And then, although I wasn't in any danger from Alfie Hymas while I was in the house, if I once stepped into the darkness of the village I would be an easy victim.

I could tell my dad everything, I supposed, and let him take over. But I knew that was no good. My dad would have had the village raised straight off. This had to be done secretly, and no one was less secretive than my dad.

But there was Will Martin. He was a man who had had a lot of experience, and he was a man who could do things quietly. I felt I could rely on him. And he had a car. If he would agree to take me across to the island we could get Fordie back easily.

'I'm going up to bed, Mam,' I said.

'Aye, I think you should. I'll bring a cup of cocoa up later on.'

'No, Mam. I don't want anything. I'll be asleep.'

'Suit yourself then, lad.'

I went out into the passage leaving them together, my dad with his back to the telly, crouched forward and fire-gazing, Mam sitting watching, knitting a jumper, the needles clicking. I walked heavily upstairs, and then very lightly down. I took my coat off the peg in the hall and went outside and drew the door softly to behind me.

It was moonlight, but fitful, for there were heavy clouds and a stiff wind pushing them evenly across the sky. But just then the harbour was white with light and the *Night Wind* was gaunt and frosted over as she lay on the beach.

I hesitated in the doorway. Along towards Ridley's corner someone leaned on the harbour wall looking down at the *Night Wind*. Was it Alfie Hymas? I couldn't make out in the light of the street lamps. A car started up at Ridley's corner. It reminded me of something – the night Fordie disappeared. That was it. Half past nine, a car had started up there. It must have been Will Martin's. He was on his way back to Shields. Fordie might have got a lift from him. But wouldn't Will Martin have said so before now?

The person by the harbour wall turned and started walking towards me, and at the same time I heard the last bus coming down into the village. I stood still as the figure came nearer.

'That John Watt there?'

It was Andy Armstrong. Just for a second he seemed threatening and dangerous. Then I got a grip of myself. I was letting my imagination run away with me.

'It's me, Mr Armstrong.'

'What you up to?'

'Just getting some air.'

'Come and walk up the point with me then. I'm going on duty.'

'I can't. I have to go back in.'

'Suit yourself.'

After he'd gone I stepped out into the street. Alfie Hymas was leaning against the harbour wall, his back to me, looking down on the *Night Wind*.

I started towards Sea Lonnen. As I passed the old shed I heard voices and the shuffling of feet. In the shadows, a cigarette glowed. I shivered a bit. It could almost be the ghosts of the two Bobs reliving the things they'd known best on earth. A big cloud over the moon smothered the harbour in darkness again.

There were quick footsteps behind me as I started up Sea Lonnen, and as I reached Will Martin's gate somebody was there behind me, a very strong presence with a very strong smell of scent.

'What do you want this time of night, John Watt? Are you coming to our house?'

It was Linda Martin, sounding very grown-up.

'I wanted to have a word with your dad.'

'Well, I don't know whether he's in.'

'He's not going off on a trip yet.'

'You know everything, don't you?'

She put a key in the lock of the front door.

'Been into Alnwick?' I asked.

'To a dance. You wait here.'

Light from the living-room fell across the small hallway as she went in, a hallway that was carpeted and had a shiny hallstand and a picture in it, and wasn't bare walls and lino like ours.

I heard her voice, high and happy inside, and her mother's and then Will Martin's. The door opened again, and Will Martin came out.

'John Watt, is it? Can I help you, lad?'

The smoke of his pipe hung strongly on the night air. It was reassuring.

'Mr Martin, it's about Fordie Telford.'

He started to stroll down to the gate and I followed him.

'Still on that tack, John? Made some discoveries?'

'Well, in a way. But I wanted to ask you a question. I want you to help me. You're the only one I can ask.'

Will Martin leaned on the gate and looked out to sea where lights of a ship passed slowly through the darkness. The wind rustled through the bushes in the garden.

'Ask away, lad.'

'Mr Martin. I know where Fordie Telford is.'

'So do we all. He went down with the coble.'

'No he didn't. He wasn't in the coble. He was down at Shields.'

'Now then, John, you're having me on, aren't you? We've been over all this . . .'

'Mr Martin, you have to believe me. That deckie-learner from the *Mayflower* today, he told me he saw Fordie at Shields the night the coble was lost.'

'I thought there was some doubt about that.'

That surprised me. 'You've heard what happened to Charlie? He was threatened to make him deny what he told me. But it's true what he told me, all the same. This is a dangerous business, Mr Martin.'

'So let's say the Telford boy *wasn't* in the coble. Ran

away instead. In that case the police should be told and a search made for him. I suppose you've no idea where he was going?'

'No, Mr Martin. But I know where Fordie is.'

He stood still, and his hand grasped my shoulder.

'What do you mean?'

'I know where he is. I've seen him.'

'Alive?'

'Yes. He was unconscious, but alive.'

He didn't say anything. And suddenly I made my mind up.

'He's ill and he's frightened. He's frightened of somebody or something in this village. But I think he should be got to a hospital and Jim Pollard told the facts ...'

'Yes, of course. Pollard must be told. And the boy taken to hospital. What do you want me to do?'

'I'll have to explain properly ...'

'Aye?'

'The Thursday night Fordie Telford disappeared and the coble was lost, you went off on a trip.'

'That's right.'

'And you went down to Shields by car?'

'Aye.'

'Leaving Rudharbour about half past nine?'

'Aye.'

'Mr Martin – did you give Fordie Telford a lift down to Shields?'

He didn't answer me. He stood still looking out to sea. I wondered whether he hadn't heard me. But he must have.

'Mr Martin ...'

'Don't you think I would have said so if I'd given the boy a lift?' He was quite brusque then.

'Well, he must have gone to Shields in your car. It was the only way. And I'll tell you something else. I think he stowed away in your ship – in the *Jenny Mary*.'

For a moment he said nothing, then he sighed, knocked his pipe out against the wall so that the ashes from it fell glowing on to the ground, and said,

'You'd better tell me what you're thinking. We'll walk a bit.'

So we paced backwards and forwards up and down the Sea Lonnen while I explained what I thought Fordie had done. Fordie was a quick thinker. He could have got into that car without Will Martin knowing he was there. Will Martin used to back his car out of the garage, then get out to close the garage doors, and Fordie could have got in behind the back seat while he was doing that. And it wouldn't have been beyond him to nip out without being seen at Shields. A stowaway right from the start. And wasn't it likely, then, that he stowed away in the *Jenny Mary*? She was the only other vessel going north from Shields that night. And if that was so, mightn't he have seen what happened to the coble?

'All you tell me could possibly have happened, though I knew nothing of it. But I still don't understand – where is he now? And what do you mean by him seeing what happened to the coble?'

'I should warn you, Mr Martin, first of all, that it's dangerous for you to be talking to me and for you to help me.'

To my surprise he laughed. He laughed loud but not very long, as if he didn't want to hurt my feelings by laughing but couldn't help it.

'John,' he said, 'you've made some remarkable discoveries. Now tell me, who is it we're in danger from?'

'Alfie Hymas.' He said nothing to that, so I went on, 'I think it was Alfie Hymas cut the nets of the *Night Wind*. I think he did it because he'd quarrelled with the two Bobs and wanted to teach them a lesson. He didn't mean to capsize them – he didn't expect that, but it happened. And he was afraid to own up. But I think Fordie saw it from the deck of the *Jenny Mary* . . .'

'I see. That's quite a reconstruction, John. You are a remarkable boy.' His voice was quiet, but he meant what he said, I could tell, and I felt very proud just then. 'But Alfie Hymas, now. I wouldn't have thought it of Alfie Hymas. After all, he was a close relative of the two Bobs.'

'I know that,' I said quickly, 'and I don't mean he sank the coble deliberately. I think it was all an accident – he's a man with a quick temper . . .'

'And the luck ran out for him? Aye. It's a funny thing. For some men, no matter how they try, the luck seems to turn against them. Things twist in their hands. You have to be careful about everything you do, everything you start. Once the luck runs out for the first time, it does it again and again . . .' He seemed to be speaking to himself not me, but then he went on more briskly, 'Where is the Telford boy and what do you want me to do?'

'He's on Holy Island.'

'The island? Yes. Of course.'

'Well, if you would take me in your car we could get across to the island and back before high tide. We could just make it. And we could go straight to Jim Pollard then. You see, I must get Fordie to the policeman quickly and without Alfie Hymas seeing him. If we were in your car . . .'

'Yes of course, I'll go across for the boy. But wouldn't

you be safer staying at home maybe, till I bring him back?'

'No, that's no good. He's with Holy Island Joe and the old man won't give him up to anybody but me.'

We went by the narrow road that led by the sea behind the sand dunes, a winding dark road, but Will Martin was a good driver and he drove fast.

When we were on the causeway that led across to the island, Will Martin stopped the car.

'It's coming in fast,' he said. And it was true that the water was spreading silently over the marshy flats at each side and a narrow stream was flowing across the causeway at its centre.

'We can still make it, Mr Martin. If we're quick enough.'

He took the brake off and we went across.

Joe opened the door when I knocked, peering out into the darkness at us.

'Who is it?' he asked.

'It's me, Joe.'

'John Watt? How did you get here? Have you taken to using wings?'

'Joe, I've come to take Fordie to hospital.'

'Fordie? What for? The lad's fine. You had better come in. And the man with you.'

Joe's cottage was tiny, and the three of us seemed to fill the small front room. Joe turned up the oil lamp and stirred the fire and then sat down on the settle, his gnarled hands at rest on his knees, his silver eyes gazing at Will Martin.

'Joe, this is Skipper Will Martin. He's brought me in his car and he'll take Fordie to hospital if we're quick.'

'Hold on a minute, John Watt. Always in too much of a

hurry. Comes through relying on your brain too much, John Watt. Not enough on your instinct. Haven't I told you that before?'

'But, Joe, the tide...'

'Aye. But we'll bide a while yet. Will Martin, eh? I seem to remember the name. Were you the skipper of the *Northumbrian Maid*?'

# 14

I'd been fidgeting about restlessly, but when Joe said that I was still enough. I looked at Will Martin's face and he had a bitter smile on it.

'You've a good memory, old man.'

'Some things you don't forget.'

'No. That's true. Some things are never forgotten. People won't let them be.'

'You were skipper when she was lost?'

'Aye.'

'But the court exonerated you.'

'The *court* did,' he replied, making reservations. I knew what he meant. The men of the village, the two Bobs, hadn't. And neither had Alfie. 'It was bad luck. No skipper would willingly risk his ship and his men.'

'The man in the glass cage,' Joe muttered. 'The man pursued by what he's pursuing. Standing here with us.' And then he spoke up. 'So, you've come to take the lad to hospital, John Watt? Why, maybe it's not a bad idea. He's come round, so he should be able to make the journey. Come on, we'll get him out of his bed. Mebbe you could be getting your car turned round, Mr Martin.'

I followed the old man upstairs in a daze. I couldn't get over it. Will Martin the skipper of the *Northumbrian Maid* – the man who'd lost his ship and most of her crew, and lost them because he took that extra risk that he shouldn't have taken. I remembered what he'd said about the luck running out, things twisting in a man's hand. I'd thought he meant Alfie Hymas, but he hadn't. He'd been talking about himself. Will Martin, the man I'd always admired, had that on his conscience.

Fordie was sitting up in bed. He still looked pale and dazed, but he recognized me. 'Hi, John,' he said.

'Hi, Fordie. How's it going?'

'I'm all right now.' But he looked round the room fearfully. 'I can't get it clear where I am and how I got here. And who's he?'

He meant Joe. Joe ignored this and sat down.

'What's come over you, John Watt? Why have you brought yon man here?'

'I didn't know! Honest – I've just realized...'

'Will you never learn, John Watt?'

'It's all very well for you to talk, but I didn't know about the *Northumbrian Maid*. I didn't have all the facts! People don't tell me things...'

'Will you never learn to trust your instincts instead of your intellect, John Watt? Can you not smell it? Can you not smell the fear on him? Do you know what he's planning?'

'But Will Martin! I never thought...'

I shivered as I sat there, for I could see he was right. I'd been blind as a bat not to realize it before. If you took it that Alfie Hymas had been telling the truth and hadn't gone as far north as the Farnes, then the only ship that could have swamped the coble was the *Jenny Mary*. And Will Martin – he had good reason for hating the two Bobs. I thought he ignored what they said about him, but it could be that their remarks went deep, tormenting him, stopping him from forgetting what he had on his conscience. Maybe he only meant to scare the two Bobs a bit, or annoy them by cutting their nets, but not capsize them. Maybe it all went further than he intended and he was landed with their deaths on his conscience also.

Would he not want to clear that burden? Not by confessing – he'd had time for that – but by getting rid of those who knew? He'd been at Shields that day. He knew what Charlie had told me. He could have threatened him. And if Fordie had been in the *Jenny Mary*, he must have seen what happened to the *Night Wind* – and he would have good reason for fearing Will Martin. The old man was right. I'd led us – all three of us – right into a trap.

The crack skipper, they called him. The crack skipper! That must have hurt. He must never have taken out another trawler after the loss of *Northumbrian Maid*. He must have given up fishing, taken a job as master of a small steamer.

I'd never even begun to understand Will Martin.

'Fear and guilt. Fear and guilt,' muttered Joe.

Fordie was looking worried. 'What's he on about?' he asked.

I heard the car turning outside.

'Joe. We can't go with him,' I said.

'We can. Leave it to me. You wait and watch for my signal, John Watt, then you run as you've never run with this lad, and get away off the island.'

I turned to Fordie. 'Look, Fordie, you have to trust me and do what I say. All right? It'll seem a bit strange, what we're going to do, but it'll be all right. So come on, you'd better get some clothes on . . .'

The lights of Will Martin's car cautiously probed the darkness as we drove towards the causeway, for the moon was hidden again.

'I can hardly make out the road,' he said. 'Are we going the right way?'

'Keep left, man, left,' Joe said.

I couldn't stop shivering, partly with cold, partly with fear. Fordie, sitting beside me in the back seat, started suddenly at the sound of Will Martin's voice. When we bundled him into the car I don't think he saw Will Martin at all. I could feel him go tense beside me, and I put my hand firmly on his arm.

The roughness of the road seemed to have gone from under the tyres. We seemed to be driving on sand.

'Are you sure we're right, old man?' asked Will Martin. 'We're not on the road.'

'I know the way, don't worry. The old Pilgrim's Way. We follow the stakes. The sand is firm enough to take the car. And it's the quickest way. Quicker than yon causeway.'

'All the same ...' Will Martin began, and then the car stopped. 'Quickest way! We're bogged down in the sand!' He revved the engine and the wheels bit farther into the damp sand.

'We've missed the stakes then,' said Joe. 'We'd best get out and push, eh? And we'd best be quick. The tide's rising. You two young-uns – come on.'

There was a dull glow from the clouds lighting the flat waste of the slakes, and the spreading waters that covered the slakes were creeping forward, almost to the car.

'Joe – the tide's well up!' I exclaimed.

'We must push hard then.'

We put our shoulders to the back of the car, Will Martin still at the wheel.

'Go now, John Watt,' said Joe quietly.

'But Joe . . .'

'Don't argue. Go.'

I grabbed Fordie and we started to run. He still wasn't well and he staggered. I had to drag him along over the wet sand. I wasn't sure of the direction, but I ran from the creeping sea to where I thought the causeway was. We might still get across before the tide was too high.

'John – that fellow – Will Martin . . .' panted Fordie.

'Save your breath,' I said.

A low mist lay across the land as we reached the causeway. It blurred and hid the lines of the land. Our footsteps rang loud on the road as we ran. And we hadn't got on to the causeway when we heard footsteps behind us, and I knew who it would be. So did Fordie. We stood for a moment, listening, panting loud, then we ran on. I was afraid for Joe.

On either side of the causeway the water was deep now, swirling steadily forward over the slakes towards the island, and there was mist in soft patches here and there, and the distant sound of the main stream as it went swiftly through the deepest channel in the centre. As we reached it, the moon came out, and we stopped dead, hesitating before that tide that was foaming deep across the path.

'I'm stopping here! I'm not risking it!' Fordie panted. We looked back. There was the dark figure of Will Martin running towards us. We had to risk it. I could see now that if we died and Joe died, Will Martin could easily explain away that tragedy in these circumstances.

I grabbed Fordie's arm and pulled him and we ran on

together into the water. We splashed in and it was deepening fast, the tide swirled and pulled about our knees, then about our thighs.

'Hold on, Fordie!' I yelled above the noise of the water, but he stumbled and went under, and I remember shouting and crying as I stooped down, pulling him to his feet again. 'Stay in the middle!' I yelled, because the real danger was if you went off the causeway into the hollows and pools at each side.

We reached the middle where the refuge box loomed up white in the moonlight, and I had a glimpse of the deeper water coming in from the sea in a fierce determined roll towards us. We would never get across.

I got Fordie to the steps of the refuge box and we got ourselves up and inside and pulled the door shut. There was a bench there and Fordie fell on to it. Our lungs were bursting, and the sound of our gasping drowned the roar of the water beneath. I went to the window after a bit to look out for Will Martin. If he found us there we wouldn't have a chance to escape.

I saw him at last running towards us out of the mist, splashing through the water. I saw straight away he didn't have a chance. His coat was hampering him, and he was moving over towards the right. Any minute now he would be off the path and into the main tide. I couldn't see him running straight to his death like that. In spite of everything that had happened I felt Will Martin had been more unfortunate than anything else. I pulled open the door of the refuge box and shouted to him, 'Watch out! Keep to the left!'

Above the sound of the sea and the wind he must have heard me, for he looked up in our direction. And doing that he somehow lost his balance. We saw him fall and go under, and scramble up and fall again, and we saw the tide swirling about him, carrying him on over the slakes towards the sea.

The luck had left Will Martin for the last time.

# 15

I'll never forget the night we spent in that refuge box with the sea only a few feet beneath us, and the mist and darkness all round. It seemed as if the night would go on for ever and the tide would never ebb.

Fordie told me, as it came back to him, what had happened the night he disappeared, and I found I'd been right in the main in my reconstruction. Of course, I knew then that I'd been wrong over the most important conclusion. And yet I'd got everything else right. Fordie had meant to run away. It was Will Martin passing that gave him the idea to do it then. He'd hidden in Will Martin's car, and he had seen Charlie at Shields, and when he couldn't get on to a ship he'd stowed away in the *Jenny Mary* knowing he could probably get ashore somewhere in Scotland. When they were well at sea, he'd come out, meaning to tell Will Martin what he'd done and ask him to put him ashore at the first port of call. Will had been on the bridge, and Fordie had gone up to him, and just at that moment he'd seen the *Night Wind* signalling to the *Jenny Mary* to move over, and he'd seen the look on Will's face, and he'd known he meant to cut the nets. Fordie had shouted to him, and Will Martin turned, and the nets were crossed and there were cries from the coble as she was towed along and then capsized. Fordie ran to the side and peered over, but then he could see nothing in the darkness. He knew they were passing the Farnes, and realizing Holy Island was near and that he would be in danger from Will Martin, he didn't stop to think. He pulled off his boots and dived overboard. I suppose the shock and the long swim had affected his memory. Anyway, he remembered nothing after that except a terrible fear.

I thought then about Will Martin, and what he'd said about luck and things twisting in a man's hands. I could see that the affair of the *Northumbrian Maid* had ruined his life, and the Hymases would never let him forget. So he tried to cut their nets that night just to get his own back. And then, when he saw their coble capsize I suppose he felt he couldn't own up to what he'd done, he couldn't have a second scandal and people bringing up what happened to the *Northumbrian Maid* all over again. He was pursued all right. I wondered whether he meant to kill me and Fordie. He was a strange man, I thought. A man you couldn't say was bad or good. The facts weren't straight. They didn't fit. In spite of everything, I was sorry about Will Martin that night.

Then the mist cleared and the moon came out to show us the sea all round, but it wasn't till dawn that the tide went down. We stumbled out of the box and turned back to the island.

We saw Will Martin's car, a black lump amidst the greyness, and then we ran because there was something huddled on the sand by its wheels. Joe was hardly breathing and he was wet through, seaweed and sand on his clothes and in his hair and beard. The tide had reached that far, but not far enough or strong enough to carry him away, for the wheels of the car had saved him from that. There were no gulls that morning about the old man.

I left Fordie with him and ran to the phone box and told Jim Pollard as much as was necessary to make him get out to us with an ambulance. Then I got into Joe's cottage through a window and collected all the blankets I could carry. When the ambulance came grinding along in the dawn, Fordie and I were sitting on the sand huddled in a blanket and Joe lay still beside us, his face turned up to the sun.

As they were carrying him to the ambulance, he opened his eyes and saw me. His lips moved and I bent to listen.

'Yon skipper,' he whispered. 'Yon skipper. Let him keep his secret, lad.'

I knew straight off what he meant. We had come to an understanding, Joe and me.

We were taken back to Rudharbour. We got there about nine o'clock. My mam and dad had sat up all night worried out of their wits because they didn't know where I was, but Jim Pollard had passed on the news as soon as I'd phoned him, so my mam and old Mrs Telford were waiting with blankets and hot drinks and beaming smiles to welcome us. My dad, of course, had had to catch the bus to go for his medical.

It was a happy day, I suppose, with Fordie back safe. And then my dad comes home later with the news that his pension was to be the same.

'What about that, our John? No better, no worse. Common mean, that's me!'

It wasn't easy for me to persuade Fordie to say nothing about Will Martin's part in the loss of the coble. He was all for having justice done. But in the end I persuaded him. The Hymases were gone and so was Will Martin. There was no point in bringing the old scandal to light again and starting off a new one that hurt people still living. So Will Martin was looked on as a bit of a hero – a man who'd lost his life trying to help me bring Fordie home off the island. And when his body was recovered from the sea a while later by Amble way I went to the funeral at the chapel without any grumbling. I felt sorry for Mrs Martin and Linda and for Will Martin whom the luck had turned against, but I was pleased nobody else knew it had turned.

I owed a lot to Holy Island Joe, apart from my life and Fordie's. I understood myself better because of Joe. I understood it was foolish to let my own conceit in myself blind me to the truth. That was one thing. And I understood what he meant by fear and guilt. I felt guilty where Alfie Hymas was concerned. But I went and apologized to him. He's all right is Alfie Hymas. We're good friends now. But most of all, I felt guilty where Joe was concerned. If I'd been a bit wiser, a bit less blind, I would never had got Joe mixed up in a struggle with Will Martin.

But I kept my promise to Joe. Every week-end in October and all of half-term I was out in the island, and watching the migrants. And by that time I had the evidence and I could prove his theory was right. The migrants were on their way south, and they only stopped over on the island when visibility round about was bad, and when visibility improved they were off again.

I would come and see Joe and tell him how things were going, and when I had it finished I went and showed it all to him – the graphs and the charts and everything – and explained it.

I think he understood and I think it made him happy, but I couldn't really tell. His eyes were fierce and silver as ever, but something had happened to Joe in the fight with Will Martin, and the old man couldn't speak or move at all after that day. He would lie on a bed pushed into the window of the cottage, watching the gulls as they perched on his garden wall, his fierce eyes calling them fools, and watching the October mists and storms. But he was gone from there before the robin left the thorn hedge on New Year's day.

If you have enjoyed this book and would like to know about others which we publish, why not join the Puffin Club? You will receive the club magazine, *Puffin Post*, four times a year and a smart badge and membership book. You will also be able to enter all the competitions. For details send a stamped addressed envelope to: